THE COMPLETE BOOK OF CHRISTIAN

Wedding Vows

THE IMPORTANCE OF HOW YOU SAY "I DO"

· H. NORMAN WRIGHT ·

BETHANY HOUSE PUBLISHERS

Minneapolis, Minnesota

The Complete Book of Christian Wedding Vows
Copyright © 2001
H. Norman Wright

Cover design by David Uttley Design. Interior design by Eric Walljasper

Published by Bethany House Publishers
A Ministry of Bethany Fellowship International
11400 Hampshire Avenue South, Bloomington, Minnesota 55438
www.bethanyhouse.com

Printed in the United States of America

Library of Congress Cataloging-in-Publication Data

Wright, H. Norman.
    The complete book of Christian wedding vows : the importance of how you say "I do" / by H. Norman Wright.
        p. cm.
    ISBN 07642-2411-5 (hardback : alk. paper)
    1. Marriage—Religious aspects—Christianity. 2. Weddings. 3. Vows. I. Title.
    BV835 .W736 2001
    265'.5—dc21

                                                   00-012102

H. NORMAN WRIGHT, a licensed marriage, family, and child therapist, is the founder and director of Christian Marriage Enrichment. He is the author of over sixty books on a variety of subjects, including *Before You Say "I Do,"* a marriage preparation manual for couples, and *The Perfect Catch* (Bethany House Publishers), a collection of sixty devotional readings for fishermen. He and his wife, Joyce, have been married for over forty years and live in Long Beach, California.

Contents

How to Use This Book

Congratulations on your upcoming wedding! From that day on, you and your groom- or bride-to-be will be sharing the rest of your lives together.

As Christians, you want a ceremony that reflects your commitment to each other, to God, and to marriage itself. You want a wedding that is unique, meaningful, memorable.

The heart of the service (and of this book) is the vows you will make to each other. These will be some of the most important words you will ever say. Spoken before family, friends, and God, they express a lifelong pledge of love and faithfulness.

In my years as a premarital counselor, I've met with countless couples who desired personalized, Christ-honoring vows but wanted help in creating them. That's what this book is all about.

You will find step-by-step advice for adding a unique touch to your vows and indeed, the entire ceremony. For example, the chapter "How to Create Your Vows" directs questions to you and your future spouse that will help you identify possible themes and phrases you would like expressed in your own wedding vows. In the same way, "Vows for Inspiration" and other examples throughout the book can be used as a starting point. If you like parts of a vow, feel free to personalize it and add your own.

Also included is a special chapter for married couples who want to reaffirm their vows, as well as a chapter for writing vows that include others, such as parents or children from a previous marriage.

To personalize other elements of a wedding ceremony, there are meaningful Scripture readings, prayers, quotations, and poems. In addition, I have provided ideas for involving your guests so that they are not just passive spectators.

As you read on, keep in mind that it's important to talk with your pastor about your vows and the entire ceremony. Your church or denomination may have a standard order of service and perhaps even acceptable variations. However, by working together and perhaps even sharing this book and its biblical options, personal touches can be added to virtually any ceremony.

Finally, after you have created the perfect vows for your wedding, be sure to record them in the back of this book where they can be reread and relived at each anniversary or special moment in your marriage.

You first heard it when you were a child. "Now, I want you to promise me…"

"…you'll listen to your older sister."

"…you won't get into the cookies."

"…you'll come right home from school."

"…you'll be good for Grandma."

Of course, these types of promises weren't always freely given. You were "requested" to make them.

As you grew up, you might have learned to "use" promises yourself: "I promise…really," or "Hey, *you promised!*" or "Please promise me you won't tell." Promises eventually become an important part of friendships, showing trust. You even might have exchanged a promise ring with a special friend.

Simply stated, a promise is an agreement to do something or not to do something. The word *promise* or *promised* appears in Scripture over a hundred times. In Psalm 15, David reveals the incredible value of keeping a promise:

> *Lord, who may go and find refuge and shelter in your tabernacle up on your holy hill? Anyone who leads a blameless life and is truly sincere. Anyone who refuses to slander others, does not listen to gossip, never harms his neighbor, speaks out against sin, criticizes those committing it, commends the faithful followers of the Lord,* keeps a promise even if it ruins him, *does not crush his debtors with high interest rates, and refuses to testify against the innocent despite the bribes offered him—such a man shall stand firm forever* (vv. 1-5 TLB, emphasis added).

When you make a promise, you're saying, "Trust me. You can depend on me. I will follow through." It's not just an agreement on your part, it's a commitment. And until this point, every promise volunteered on your part—whether freely given or asked of you—was just the prelude to the promise you are going to make on your wedding day.

The details of a wedding ceremony—the processional music, the attendants, the seating of the parents, the flowers, the words of the minister, the food at the reception—are important, but you could have all of the above and still not be married. *The heart of your wedding will be your vows!* Sadly, I've talked to many couples that never gave any thought to the vows until either the rehearsal or the actual wedding.

It's not just making your wedding memorable with heartfelt vows—it's that your vows express what you will be doing with the rest of your life together!

The language of a wedding service should be the language of promising. That's why the ceremony has such a serious ring to it. The promises are to be spoken seriously and without coercion. And once you make these promises through the exchanging of vows, you and your spouse will never be the same. You will move to a new life status by virtue of your promising. A transformation will take place. What was separate before will now become "one flesh." And no matter what happens, this fact can never be erased.

Promises have a future quality about them as well. A promise is only kept when it's fulfilled. A promise is not contingent upon changes in the future. It's not "I promise, if…"

There are no conditions. This is not a contract. A contract contains conditional clauses. Both parties are responsible for carrying out their part of the pact. There are conditional or "if" clauses: If you do this, the other person must do this, and if the other person does this, you must do this. But in the marriage relationship there are no conditional clauses. It's an unconditional commitment. And each day of your marriage you will need to renew your act of commitment to your partner.

VOWS FOR INSPIRATION

The following are the creative vows of Colleen Nelson and Joel Blomenkamp, who were married in 1995. They waited seven long years to marry, since they were determined to graduate from college first.

Colleen: *Joel, I stand before you today, honored and excited as I am about to become your wife. I thank the Lord for the enduring and patient love He has given us these past seven years. You are a loving, gentle, and kind man. You're devoted and committed to serving others and the Lord. You are the love of my life, and I am so blessed with the gift of spending the rest of my life with you.*

As we become husband and wife today, I promise to love you with an unending and unconditional love. I will honor and respect you, comfort and cherish you. May I bring you good, not harm, all the days of my life. I will stand by you and submit to you as God guides us to do His will.

I will be with you in sickness and in health, whether we are rich or poor, and during the times when we are filled with joy and when we are filled with sorrow. I will not leave you.

Joel, I will be yours alone as long as God allows us to live.

Joel: *Today I have come to commit my love to you. Although I come with a fallible love, I promise to strive to love you as Christ has loved the church. I promise to cherish you in* times of joy and despair, to care for you when you are sick and in health, to hope with you now and forever, to protect you and not to harm you, to love you and to forsake all others.

I promise to love you as Scripture commands me to: "for love is patient, love is kind. It does not envy, it does not boast, it is not proud. It is not rude, it is not self-seeking, it is not easily angered, it keeps no record of wrongs. Love does not delight in evil, but rejoices with the truth. It always protects, always hopes, always perseveres. Where there are prophecies, they will cease; where there are tongues, they will be stilled, where there is knowledge, it will pass away, but love…love never fails. And now these three remain: Faith, Hope, and Love, but the greatest of these is Love."

Although calamity and darkness may surround us, I promise to be here when you need me. Although the world values "being in love," I promise to love you even if the feelings of love go away. Before our friends and family, before you, and before my Lord and Savior, I commit these promises to you.

A Christian marriage goes beyond an earthly partnership. It's a commitment involving three individuals—husband, wife, and Jesus Christ.

> *One standing alone can be attacked and defeated, but two can stand back-to-back and conquer; three is even better, for a triple-braided cord is not easily broken* (Ecclesiastes 4:12 TLB).

Commitment means many things to different people. For some, the strength of their commitments varies with how they feel emotionally or physically. However, true commitment is not based primarily on feelings. A promise is a binding pledge, a pledge of mutual fidelity and mutual submission. It is a private pledge you also make public. It is a pledge carried out to completion, running over any roadblocks. It is a total giving of oneself to another person. Yes, it is risky, but it makes life fulfilling.

Commitment means giving up the childish dream of being unconditionally accepted by your partner, who will fulfill all your needs and make up for all your childhood disappointments. It means expecting to be disappointed by the other, learning to accept this, and not using it as a reason to pull the plug.[1]

Perhaps a better way to describe this is to compare it with bungee jumping. If you've ever taken the plunge, you know that when you take that step off the platform, you are committed to follow through. There is no more time to think it over or change your mind. There is no turning back.

A friend of mine shared with me what has made his marriage last. He said, "Norm, we each had a commitment to each other and to the marriage. When our commitment to each other was low, it was the commitment to the marriage that kept us together."

When a couple comes together, it is like two rivers that merge into one. If you looked upstream at each river before they merged, you would observe that each one flowed gently along. But when they come together, watch out.

Those two nice streams come at each other with intensity. They merge in a wild commotion of froth. They seem to hit head on as if each was determined not to be dominated by the other.

But in time, you can almost see the angry whitecaps diminish and practically bow in respect to each other. It's as if they join forces since they know what's ahead of them is better.

When you look downstream you'll see the river sweeping steadily on again. It's broader there, more majestic, and gives you the feeling that something good had come out of the conflict.

This is what a good, committed marriage is like. When two independent streams of existence come together, there will probably be some clashes. Personalities rush against each other. There may be some power struggles. You wonder if this is the way it was meant to be.

It's all right. Like the two rivers, what comes out of your struggle will be something better and more powerful than what you were on your own.[2]

Perhaps you're wondering why I've included this discussion about what marriage is all about: *Why not get right on to the creation of the vows?* That's the problem. That's what most people do without really considering what they're promising.

These thoughts about marriage are not meant to discourage you or put a damper upon this wonderful anticipated event. They are shared to help you think, reflect, and move into your marriage with a sense of optimistic realism.

> "*...May I bring you good, not harm, all the days of my life. I will be yours alone as long as God allows us to live.*"

Commitment to another person until he or she dies seems idealistic to some. When it suits them and they're not inconvenienced by it, they keep it. But when certain problems occur, they think it's not valid.

Commitment is more than continuing to stick it out and suffer with a poor choice of a spouse. It's not just maintaining; it's investing. It's not just enduring; it's working to make the relationship grow. It's not just accepting and tolerating negative and destructive patterns on the part of your spouse; it's working toward change. It's sticking to someone regardless of circumstances. A wife once shared this story with me in a letter:

> In 1988, I was diagnosed with epstein-barr virus (chronic fatigue syndrome). It really changed my life, which had been filled with excitement and vibrancy. My husband, Kelly, has stood with me and become my protector through these past years of adjustment. He has taken care of our family when my strength would not allow me. He has held my hand through depression, including ten days in the hospital. He has insisted I get needed rest, even if it was more of a burden on him. He has paid the price of any hopeful cure we have found, no matter the cost. He has been more than a husband; he has been my best friend— a friend that has stayed closer than any family member. He was my "knight in shining armor" when I met him and has proven to be so throughout our fourteen and a half years of marriage. I sometimes tell him that he has been "my salvation," because I don't know that I would still be going on if it weren't for his strength. I don't know that I would still walk with the Lord if it were not for his encouragement. Knowing him has been the greatest experience.

Keep in mind there will be ups and downs throughout the life of your marriage. There will be massive changes, some predictable and others intrusive. They hold the potential for growth

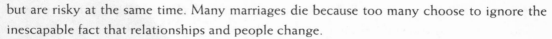

but are risky at the same time. Many marriages die because too many choose to ignore the inescapable fact that relationships and people change.

A wife shared the following story with the congregation at her son's church:

> *Since we have been married fifty years, you can just imagine how much change we have gone through: three wars, eleven presidents, five recessions, going from the Model A to the moon, from country road to the information superhighway. While these changes around us have been great, the personal changes that God has enacted within us through each other have been even greater. Although we often couldn't see how God was working in our lives at that time, we look back now and realize that our marriage has been a school of character development. God has used my husband in my life, and He's used me in his life to make us more like Christ. So what are the lessons that we've learned about how God uses marriage to change us? There are many. Through fifty years of marriage we've learned that differences develop us, that crises cultivate us, and that ministry melts us together.*
>
> *First, God has used our differences to help us grow. There have been many, many crises that God has used to develop us and to grow us. The first one was the big, big one—the crisis of being separated as soon as we got married. Ours was a wartime romance. We met at church, dated two months, got married after three weeks of engagement, and just after two months of marriage, we didn't see each other for the next two years, for Jimmy was shipped to the South Pacific during World War II. When he returned two years later, we were total strangers, but we were married to each other!*

How would you have handled that situation? How do you handle change? How do you handle the difficult, sudden, and painful changes? You've got to be willing to face the fact that changes will occur—you will change, your marriage will change, your partner will want you to change, and you will want him or her to change.[3]

Donald Harvey, author of *The Drifting Marriage*, says:

> *Making a commitment to marriage as an institution is not meant to be a sentencing. Its intent is to offer security and stability. All couples have conflicts. Every marriage has to make adjustments. Feeling secure in a mate's commitment to the marriage allows the opportunity for dealing with conflicts and for needed adjustments to occur. This is what makes marriage resilient.*
>
> *A marriage can endure many affronts, whether from within or without, if the commitment to the marriage as an institution is strong. It takes this kind of commitment for growth to occur.*[4]

Remember your commitment is a characteristic of behaving in love. For your marriage to be stable and growth to occur, commitment to both marriage as an institution and marriage as a relationship must be present. Commitment to marriage as an institution gives you a context in which growth can occur. Commitment to marriage as a relationship guarantees that the act by which a marriage is built will take place. Together, and only together, a marriage is created.[5]

What will you give up in order to marry your partner? Have you ever thought about it? Many individuals today simply try to bring their single lifestyle into their marriage relationship. They think a marriage partner is just one more addition to their already busy life. They believe they will somehow be able to fit a husband or wife in around everything else. But a rude awakening occurs when the truth of what marriage really is penetrates your life.

Sometimes commitment requires more discipline than you bargain for. Mike Mason describes it this way:

> To put it simply, marriage is a relationship far more engrossing than we want it to be. It always turns out to be more than we bargained for. It is disturbingly intense, disruptively involving, and that is exactly the way it was designed to be. It is supposed to be more, almost, than we can handle. It was meant to be a lifelong encounter that would be much more rigorous and demanding than anything human beings ever could have chosen, dreamed of, desired, or invented on their own. After all, we do not even choose to undergo such far-reaching encounters with our closest and dearest friends. Only marriage urges us into these deep and unknown waters. For that is its very purpose: to get us out beyond our depth, out of the shadows of our own secure egocentricity and into the dangerous and unpredictable depths of a real interpersonal encounter.[6]

Have you thought about what might surprise you in your marriage? Your greatest surprise may be what you discover about the person you love. There's a bit of a mystery when you marry, for no matter how well you know the other person, you still marry a stranger whom you know slightly. You know enough about them to know you love them and to believe that in time you will love and enjoy them even more. You are embarking upon a mysterious journey and unknown future.

Daphne Kingma describes marriage this way:

> In marriage we are delivered from our most ancient aloneness, embraced in the nest of human company, so that the sharp teeth of the truth that we are born and die alone are blunted by the miracle of loving companionship.

Marriage is also the incubator of love, the protected environment in which a love that is personal and touching and real can grow and, as a consequence of that growth, develop in us our highest capabilities as loving human beings. We are each still and always becoming, and when we marry, we promise not only our own becoming but also our willingness to witness and withstand the ongoing becoming of another human being. That is because in marrying we promise to love not only as we feel right now, but also as we intend to feel. In marriage we say not only, "I love you today," but also, "I promise to love you tomorrow, the next day and always."

In promising always, we promise each other time. We promise to exercise our love, to stretch it large enough to embrace the unforeseen realities of the future. We promise to learn to love beyond the level of our instincts and inclinations, to love in foul weather as well as good, in hard times as well as when we are exhilarated by the pleasures of romance.[7]

Think about this:

A marriage is not a joining of two worlds, but an abandoning of two worlds in order that one new one might be formed....

In this sense the call to be married bears comparison with Jesus' advice to the rich young man to sell all his possessions and to follow Him. It is a vocation to total abandonment. For most people, in fact, marriage is the single most wholehearted step they will ever take toward a fulfillment of Jesus' command to love one's neighbor as oneself. For every marriage partner begins as a neighbor, and often enough a neighbor who has been left beaten and wounded on the road of love, whom all the rest of the world has in a sense passed by....

The marriage vows give glory to God. While it is true that a man and a woman on their wedding day take a step toward a unique fulfillment of the commandment of love, it is even more true to say of matrimony that it is a sacramental outpouring of God's grace enabling such love to take place. The human couple indicates humbly a willingness to give themselves to this love; but it is the Lord Who makes love possible in the first place, and therefore it is He Who promises that His gift of love will not be taken away....

Marriage, even under the very best circumstances, is a crisis—one of the major crises of life—and it is a dangerous thing not to be aware of this. Whether it turns out to be a healthy, challenging, and constructive crisis or a disastrous nightmare depends largely upon how willing the partners are to be changed, how malleable they are.[8]

When you marry you will receive the love of your spouse, but at the same time you give away your freedom to think and act solely for yourself. There is great joy in receiving, but you also enter into a relationship that entails the suffering of giving. Lewis Smedes boldly states: "Anybody's marriage is a harvest of suffering.... Your marriage vow has a promise to suffer. You promised to suffer, only to suffer with, however, not from.... A marriage is a life of shared pain."[9]

The vulnerability that encompasses marriage will open your life up to a new world of hurts. Your partner can fulfill your wildest dreams or disappoint you to the extent that your relationship becomes a nightmare. At the same time, suffering might mean sharing your partner's hurt and learning how to be a source of comfort to him or her.

Marriage is a call to share every aspect of your partner's life. Perhaps you are just discovering this truth. You might have both experienced suffering when you were single, but perhaps you will experience even more in marriage. Mike Mason says, "For it is not in the nature of love to deflect pain, but rather to absorb it, and to absorb greater and greater amounts of it. Marriage gives a face to suffering, just as it gives a face to joy."[10]

How will you and your partner suffer with one another? How will you comfort one another? Think about it. Talk about it. Pray about it. The suffering will inevitably be there. Be sure your support and comfort are there as well.

Marriage is a relationship of partners. In marriage you belong to each other (1 Corinthians 7:4). Consider the following poetic definition of marriage. After you read it, share with your future spouse which portion meant the most to you.

> *I need you in my times of strength and in my weakness;*
> *I need you when you hurt as much as when I hurt.*
> *There is no longer the choice as to what we will share.*
> *We will either share all of life or be fractured persons.*
> *I didn't marry you out of need or to be needed.*
> *We were not driven by instincts or emptiness;*
> *We made a choice to love.*
> *But I think something supernatural*
> *happens at the point of marriage commitment*
> *(or maybe it's actually natural).*
> *A husband comes into existence; a wife is born.*
> *He is a whole man before and after, but at a point in*
> *time he becomes a man who also is a husband;*
> *That is—a man who needs his wife.*
> *She is a whole woman before and after.*
> *But from now on she needs him.*

She is herself but now also part of a new unit.
Maybe this is what is meant in saying,
"What God hath joined together."
Could it be He really does something special at "I do"?
Your despair is mine even if you don't tell me about it.
But when you do tell, the sharing is easier for me;
And you also can then share from my strength in that weakness.[11]

You probably have a vision for what your marriage will become. Do you have a dream? It's all right to dream, for many dreams are translated into a vision for the future and pursued in a realistic way. "Where there is no vision, the people are unrestrained" (Proverbs 29:18 NASB). Marriage itself is a dream. David Augsburger writes: "Marriage is the pursuit of a dream. A dream of loving and being loved; of wanting another and being wanted in return, of melting into another and being eagerly embraced, of understanding another and being understood, of feeling secure and guaranteeing another's security, of being fulfilled in fulfilling another's needs."[12]

Take a few moments and write out the dream you have for your marriage.

Some say dreams are just for dreamers and not for people who live in the real world. Really? The lack of dreams and visions for the future may lead to feelings of futility. Here's another poem to consider:

The Dream
may be modest or heroic,
vaguely defined or crystal clear,
a burning passion or a quiet guiding force,

a source of inspiration and strength or of corrosive conflict.
My life is enriched to the extent that
I have a Dream and give it
appropriate place in my life
—a place that is legitimate and viable
for both myself and my world.
If I have no Dream or can find no way
to live it out my life lacks
genuine purpose or meaning. [13]

As you approach the threshold of marriage, understand what you are about to promise. When you marry you are declaring that you are finding completion by taking this step. Marriage is a mysterious merging of two separate but equal individuals in such a way that they learn to complement each other and actually complete each other.

Marriage is a gift. Those who see it this way end up experiencing it as such. A gift is an item that is selected with care and consideration. Its purpose is to bring delight and fulfillment to another, an expression of deep feeling on the part of the giver.

Marriage is also a call to servanthood. Can you promise to fulfill this? It's easier to be served than to serve. Our pattern is found in this Scripture passage:

Put yourself aside, and help others get ahead. Don't be obsessed with getting your own advantage. Forget yourselves long enough to lend a helping hand. Think of yourselves the way Christ Jesus thought of himself. He had equal status with God but didn't think so much of himself that he had to cling to the advantages of that status no matter what. Not at all.

When the time came, he set aside the privileges of deity and took on the status of a slave, became human! It was an incredibly humbling process. He didn't claim special privileges. Instead, he lived a selfless, obedient life and then died a selfless, obedient death—and the worst kind of death at that: a crucifixion. Because of that obedience, God lifted him high and honored him far beyond anyone or anything—even those long ago dead and buried—will bow in worship before this Jesus Christ, and call out in praise that he is the Master of all, to the glorious honor of God the Father (Philippians 2:4-11, *The Message*).

VOWS FOR INSPIRATION

Bride: *I love you, (name). I know that you are a gift from the Lord, and I am confident that He has led us to this day.*

I commit myself, as first priority, to the Lord Jesus Christ, always seeking a more intimate relationship with Him. By His grace, I will strive to develop a gentle and quiet spirit.

I also commit myself to you. I know that you desire to please the Lord at all times, and I will seek to support you. I will seek to communicate with you openly and honestly try to share every burden.

I will also seek to encourage your leadership in our home. I commit myself to establishing our home as one of peace, godliness, and prayer. I trust in you and I joyfully become your wife today.

Groom: *(Name), I love you and I commit myself to you. I am thankful that God has called you to be my companion and friend. (Name), you know that my desire is to love and serve the Lord throughout my life, and I know that this is your goal as well. I am privileged to take you as my wife today.*

I commit myself to help and assist in seeing you become the woman God wants you to be, and I promise to lead you through this world with diligence as God gives me wisdom.

I will seek to protect you and provide for you as Christ does the church. I will care for you and cherish you, always willing to place your interests before my own.

There's More Than
One Way to
Tie the Knot

We'd like to think that our way of courtship and marriage is the best and only way. It definitely isn't, by some accounts. Even animals have their own styles of courtship, some quite similar to us humans. For example, penguins and wolves are committed to one mate for life. But not all animals share this practice.

In the world of the black widow spider, the male is considered the wimp of the species since his mate is four times larger than he is. Furthermore, only the female is glossy black; the male is white and gold.

When the male comes to court his big black beauty, he does so carefully. Though blind, the female is a sensitive, deadly huntress who knows every inch of her web by touch. The male plucks at the web deliberately like a troubadour plucking a love song on a guitar. This constant rhythm calms the female, and she waits for her lover's approach. Every few steps he plucks again so she won't respond as though he is just another insect caught in her web. Finally he reaches her, strokes her with his delicate front legs, and the mating process begins.

After mating, the male spider is exhausted and, in his weakened condition, often stumbles about the web as he tries to leave. These irregular vibrations trigger the female's hunting instinct. She not only slays her mate—thus earning her popular title—but devours him as well. So much for the wedding ceremony.

The pied hornbill is an exotic bird with an enormous beak. When it is time for hornbills to mate, the male looks for a hollow tree to convert into an apartment. After mating, the male drives the female into the tree and seals her inside by covering the entrance with mud. Talk about male domination! His mate is not allowed outside until her young are ready to leave the nest. The male shoves everything the family needs into the apartment through a small opening he has left for that purpose. Interesting! (I've seen some similarities to this style elsewhere.)

Rattlesnakes have a very intense but brief relationship. When the male finds a female during the mating season, he rises above her to his full stature and sways back and forth in a form of ballet. She responds similarly and they quickly entwine. The male then takes off, never to see his mate again. The female carries the young and gives birth, and the babies are on their own from that moment.[1] But enough about animal courtship.

How you and your future spouse courted, selected one another, and will be married likely reflects our Western culture. Almost every wedding ceremony includes customs and traditions handed down over the years. However, to make your service more unique, more personal, and more memorable, it is helpful to consider the courtship and marriage customs of other cultures, past and present. They may seem odd or different—and perhaps not appropriate in today's world—but they are shared to stretch your thinking about wedding ceremonies. Customs and traditions *are* a part of weddings. The question is, which ones do you want to keep from the past, and what new ones would you like to create?

In some cultures, wedding vows have little to do with getting married. In fact, the attitude is more like "What's love got to do with this anyway?"

Centuries ago one of the earliest means of obtaining a wife was bride capture. In fact, this is where the custom of carrying the bride over the threshold is said to have originated. Today, some cultures have created a formalized capture ritual. In certain African tribes, the future groom observes the house of the bride-to-be to discover where she sleeps. The family notices him but not officially. He returns during the evening and "captures" the willing bride while a posse of family members "chases" him at a respectful distance.

In a few societies, the economic loss experienced by the family when a woman leaves to become a bride is compensated by the exchange of a suitable gift. This could even be a sister of the groom! If you were an Olembra tribesman in Africa and wanted to be married, a wife could be "purchased" for four dogs. In the Komti caste of Bhagalpur, India, a girl is purchased in the marriage market at the rate of a hundred rupees for each year of her age. But when she reaches the age of ten, she is considered old and worthless and thus available free to anyone who wants her.

There are reasons for exchanging money for a bride. The father is being compensated for losing an economically productive member of his household. The price can also reflect the care the father exercised in raising his daughter. In some cases, if there is a questionable action on the bride's part or if she is barren, her husband can ask for a whole or prorated partial refund. (It sounds more like when you buy tires; if they wear down before they are supposed to, you get some of your payment back.)

A bride price can work the other way, however. A dowry is money or goods brought by the bride to her husband at marriage. A practice of ancient nobility, the dowry was the husband's to use, but if he died, whatever was left became the wife's. The money could also be a form of guarantee that the husband would treat his bride properly. If she were to leave his house because of cruelty, or if he divorced her, the groom would have to forfeit it.

Have you ever heard of bride service? Here is a famous example:

> *After Jacob had stayed with him for a whole month, Laban said to him, "Just because you are a relative of mine, should you work for me for nothing? Tell me what your wages should be."*
>
> *Now Laban had two daughters; the name of the older was Leah, and the name of the younger was Rachel. Leah had weak eyes, but Rachel was lovely in form, and beautiful.*

Jacob was in love with Rachel and said, "I'll work for you seven years in return for your younger daughter Rachel."

Laban said, "It's better that I give her to you than to some other man. Stay here with me." So Jacob served seven years to get Rachel, but they seemed like only a few days to him because of his love for her.

Then Jacob said to Laban, "Give me my wife. My time is completed, and I want to lie with her."

So Laban brought together all the people of the place and gave a feast. But when evening came, he took his daughter Leah and gave her to Jacob, and Jacob lay with her. And Laban gave his servant girl Zilpah to his daughter as her maidservant.

When morning came, there was Leah! So Jacob said to Laban, "What is this you have done to me? I served you for Rachel, didn't I? Why have you deceived me?"

Laban replied, "It is not our custom here to give the younger daughter in marriage before the older one. Finish this daughter's bridal week; then we will give you the younger one also, in return for another seven years of work."

And Jacob did so. He finished out the week with Leah, and then Laban gave him his daughter to be his wife. Laban gave his servant girl Bilhah to his daughter Rachel as her maidservant. Jacob lay with Rachel also, and he loved Rachel more than Leah. And he worked for Laban another seven years (Genesis 29:14-30).

The practice of bride service was prevalent in poor societies or when the bridegroom had little money.

Another practice or custom still in place in some cultures is parental selection of marriage partners. Children can be betrothed to one another at birth. Sometimes they grow up interacting with each another, but in some cases they meet the day of the wedding.

Recently a Chinese woman at our church told me about her grandparents who had met *on their wedding day*. They just celebrated their seventy-second anniversary! They weren't prompted into marriage by love, but the love developed later.

Let's imagine for a moment that you lived in the sixteenth century—the time of the Renaissance and the Reformation. Many greats of the period, including Montaigne, Erasmus, and Luther, believed a marriage should be determined by someone other than the participants. How would that go over in our society today? Marriage then was considered a duty, and your choice needed to be made on rational grounds (forget love). Fortunately, many parents made every effort to make sure their own son or daughter was pleased with the choice.

William Shakespeare brought a different perspective to marriage: love. Perhaps that's why his plays have remained so popular. He proposed that love is the true basis of a relationship, and a declaration of love was the same as a marriage proposal. Perhaps that would affect how quickly we say "I love you" to another person today!

Shakespeare was very vocal against the arranged, loveless marriages of the time. In *The Merry Wives of Windsor*, Slender, who is being urged to marry by his cousin, Shallow, responds to the question as to whether he can love the girl:

> *I will marry her, sir, at your request; but if there be no great love in the beginning, yet heaven may decrease it upon better acquaintance, when we are married and have more occasion to know one another. I hope, upon familiarity will grow contempt. But if you say, "Marry her," I will marry her; that I am freely dissolved and dissolutely.*[2]

In Shakespeare's plays, the lovers usually fall in love at first sight but never give in to their passion until they have pledged themselves to one another.

Even though Juliet was full of passion for Romeo, she said,

> *If that thy bent of love be honorable,*
> *Thy purpose marriage, send me word tomorrow,*
> *By one that I'll procure to come to thee.*
> *Where and what time thou wilt perform the rite.*[3]

Shakespeare's message that the young should marry whomever they wanted and not go along with their parents' wishes was presented in *A Midsummer Night's Dream, The Winter's Tale, The Merry Wives of Windsor, The Taming of the Shrew*, and *Romeo and Juliet*.

Today, love is the prominent factor moving couples to marriage. The phrases "I love you" or "I'm in love with you" seem to be the entrance to the stage of marriage. And for most people, love means romantic love. Could you write two paragraphs describing the love you have for the one you're going to marry?

VOWS FOR INSPIRATION

Bride: *(Name), I love you so much! For years I prayed that God would lead me to His perfect choice for a lifetime partner, and I feel confident that His will is being fulfilled today. God prepared me for this marriage, and it is only by His grace and His power working within me that I can pledge to honor, encourage, and comfort you. I pledge to remain faithful to you despite the pressures of the present and the uncertainties of the future. I promise to love and serve you. As Christ serves the church, so I will strive to serve you. I, (name of bride), am delighted to take you, (name of groom), as my helpmate and husband. This is the beginning of a brand-new Christ-centered journey and our future is as bright as the promises of God.*

Groom: *(Name), you have become so dear to me! Your love has rebuilt and transformed my life. Today I pledge my love and devotion to you with three lifelong commitments: First, I promise, by the grace of God to live an authentic Christian life: first by honoring God, and second by honoring you in all I say and do. Second, I promise to respect you. To respect you for the wisdom and intelligence you bring to our relationship, for your magical ability to create and nurture joy, and for your insatiable desire to grow by living life to its fullest. Lastly, I promise to be worthy of your trust by being trustworthy. Sweetheart, the night I proposed you said to me, "You mean you're not going away? Ever?" (Name), today that is, in fact, my solemn pledge.*

Not only is there diversity in how people select marriage partners, but wedding customs vary greatly around the world.

If you were a man interested in taking a bride on the island of Saint Kilda in the Hebrides, Scotland, you would have to undergo a grueling premarital test. Before marrying your fiancée, you would have to climb atop Lover's Rock and stand on one leg at the edge of a jutting precipice. The problem is that the cliff is 850 feet above the Atlantic Ocean, and few survive if they fall.

In the Upper Nile Valley, the Acholi tribe has a strange courtship custom that may have some merit. Women must marry their husbands three times before the contract is considered legal. The three successive ceremonies are designed to curtail hasty decisions.

The Kubris tribe is very informal. As a couple all you have to do is tell others you are married. That's all it takes. In Formosa, Taiwan, a couple lives with the bride's parents until the first child is born and then you're considered married.

The sharing of food is an important part in many weddings. In our culture, this can vary from punch, coffee, and cake after the ceremony to elaborate sit-down formal dinners. It's an aftermath of tying the knot. In other cultures, food makes the ceremony official.

Native Americans such as the Navajos state that when a man and woman eat from the same bowl in front of witnesses, they are married. In the Pawnee tribe, if a woman brings food to a man in public, and he eats it, they are married. In Morocco and other countries the couple must feed each other to make the wedding official. You can see the survival of this idea in the wedding reception when the bride and groom give each other bites of the wedding cake.

When you stand in your wedding ceremony, you'll be asked to take your future spouse's hand. This is a universal custom, which even makes wedding announcements in the newspaper: "He took her hand in marriage."

In Ethiopia, the man and woman join fingers. In Burma, the right hands are joined, and in New Guinea, the couple's hands are held together by an elder of the tribe.

How would you like it if your hands were tied together during the wedding ceremony, as they are in many cultures? This is probably where the phrase "tying the knot" originated. If you lived in Portugal your hands would be tied together with the priest's shawl. Cloth and garlands of flowers are used in Burma. Parts of your clothing would be tied together in southern India. The Tavahumare Indians of Mexico would tie your hands together with a blanket; in Bengal they use a string of flowers. It may be a bit uncomfortable for some of us, but in China the bride's and groom's hair were tied together. In parts of Ethiopia and Kenya, every guest ties the knot at an Oromo wedding ceremony. The bride and groom each have a fringed wedding shawl on which guests tie a knot that will never be undone.

The shedding of tears at weddings is virtually a universal custom. Do you think you will cry at your wedding? If you do, it is more than okay, because tears express many emotions. Recently I read a comment by Max Lucado: "Crying is the utility infielder of the emotion—it covers all bases: sorrow, happiness, excitement."[4]

Of course, tears come naturally as the bride leaves her family to become part of a new family. That sadness is acknowledged in Japan, where you would wear white for the wedding, but not for the reason you think. It signifies mourning and that the bride is supposed to be sad at leaving her parents' home.

If you were a Zulu bride you wouldn't cry alone, because your female relatives would walk with you around your father's property "crying for your father's house." In Germany, they say it is good luck to cry: "A weeping bride, a happy wife." And in India, a special prayer is offered for the "crying bride."[5]

So if you find yourself crying, you're in good company.

VOWS FOR INSPIRATION

Groom: *(Name), with love I take you to be my own beloved bride, my dearest friend, my treasured companion, my wife. I promise to love you and lead you, to encourage you and care for you.*

I will lead our home as Christ leads me. As Christ does for us, I will share every part of my life with you. I will be sensitive to your needs; I will be understanding when you hurt. I will keep the secrets that you share with me. I promise to provide you with an abundance of positive encouragement, to respect your judgment, and to listen when you speak.

Most of all, (name), I promise to continue loving you without reservation as no other man on earth could love you. By God's grace and power, I will be true and faithful to you for the rest of my life. I love you.

Bride: *(Name), I love you and I am delighted to become your wife today. I am so thankful that Jesus Christ has brought us together. You are a man after God's own heart, and I am confident that you will be a loving spiritual leader.*

To love you as God does, I must rely on Him. I promise to continue my walk with Jesus Christ and, with His help and your guidance, become the woman He has called me to be.

(Name), I promise to be faithful to you, to respect and trust your decisions. I promise to submit to your leadership and look forward to making our home a place of refuge for you...a home full of laughter, joy, and prayer.

I believe in you, (name), and I am committed to our future. You are my best friend and I am privileged to become your wife today.

What Could Possibly Go Wrong?

Weddings are highlights of any family's life. They are hoped for, planned for, saved for, and remembered for years. The amount of detailed planning and coordination that precedes the event is enormous—sometimes hundreds of hours for something that may take no longer than three or four hours. Every detail and time sequence will be checked and double-checked again to make sure everything works and everyone does what they are supposed to do. Sometimes there is a wedding coordinator to oversee the details and pageantry. And for most weddings there is a rehearsal so all the flaws and problems can be identified and worked out. At least, that's what is supposed to happen.

When I meet with couples for premarital counseling, I tell them point-blank, "Expect something to go wrong at your wedding!" There is no other way to say it. A wedding has all the ingredients necessary for a disaster waiting to happen. Why? Because it involves people (amateurs), and where there are people you can expect the best laid and orchestrated plans to go astray. If you go into your wedding with the attitude that something will probably go wrong, when it does, you won't be surprised or thrown by it. You can face the situation and say to yourself, "Here you are. I knew you would be the unwelcome guest at our wedding. We never sent *you* an invitation." Then you can adjust, go to plan B, go a different direction, create a new and lasting memory, and stay (at least) reasonably calm and collected. (I can't predict how the parents will respond.)

Now that you understand what very possibly could happen, let's enjoy some of the scenarios that have created memories for other couples.

Robert Fulghum, in his book, *It Was on Fire When I Lay Down on It*, said, "Weddings seem to be magnets for mishaps and for whatever craziness lurks in family closets. In more ways than one, weddings bring out the ding-dong in everybody involved." He described a wedding in which he was plagued by a perfectionistic MOTB (mother of the bride). She seemed to drive him and everyone else up the wall with her multitude of daily phone calls and overconcern about every imaginable and unimaginable detail. This mother had a detailed production script for the wedding, and this is how he described the disaster that occurred:

Ah, the bride. She had been dressed for hours if not days. No adrenaline was left in her body. Left alone with her father in the reception hall of the church while the march of the maidens went on and on, she had walked along the tables laden with gourmet goodies and absentmindedly sampled first the little pink and yellow and green mints. Then she picked through the silver bowls of mixed nuts and ate the pecans. Followed by a cheeseball or two, some black olives, a handful of glazed almonds, a little sausage with a frilly toothpick stuck in it, a couple of shrimps blanketed with bacon, and a cracker piled with liver pâté. To wash this down—a glass of pink champagne. Her father gave it to her. To calm her nerves.

What you noticed as the bride stood in the doorway, was not her dress, but her face. White. For what was coming down the aisle was a living grenade with the pin pulled out.

The bride threw up.

Just as she walked by her mother.

And by "threw up," I don't mean a polite little ladylike urp into her handkerchief. She puked. There's just no nice word for it. I mean, she hosed the front of the chancel—hitting two bridesmaids, the groom, a ring bearer, and me.

I am quite sure of the details. We have it all on videotape. Three cameras worth. The MOTB had thought of everything.

Only two people were seen smiling. One was the mother of the groom. And the other was the father of the bride.[1]

One setting that lends itself to the possibility of uncontrollable, unthought about before-hand disastrous events are backyard or outdoor weddings. The first one I helped officiate at was at a private home in a nice neighborhood. As we began the service it wasn't more than two minutes before we had to stop. The small plane that had just taken off from a nearby airport was drowning out even the loudest speaker. Finally it departed and we were moving further into the service when a commercial jet took off, not only drowning us out but shaking the ground as well. Everyone by this time began to look at one another and laugh. Finally we could hear again, but within a few minutes an enormous flock of blackbirds flew into one of the trees and proceeded to chatter. I'm not sure which was worse—the birds or the jet!

By this time it was late morning in early summer in Southern California. You guessed it! The temperature was rising! It was getting warm—quite warm—and the other officiating minister and I were in suits. I hoped the sweat wasn't too obvious as it began to trickle down our foreheads.

The payoff, though, was the dog. Not an ordinary dog, but one of those dorky, prissy types. It looked like a small, detached mop. It ambled out and headed for, you guessed it, the main grouping—the two of us conducting the service and the bride and groom. It stood between us, first looking at the bride and groom and then my friend and me. Now, you've got to understand the dynamics here. My friend Rex and I have worked together for years teaching and conducting seminars together. We know how one another thinks and we kid and joke around a lot. At this point with the dog looking back and forth, I knew what Rex was thinking and he knew what I was thinking: "Is that dog going to hike his leg or not?" I didn't dare look at Rex or we both would have doubled over with laughter since this dog was the last straw. And the look on the bride's and groom's faces confirmed that a similar thought had crossed their minds as well.

Fortunately we got through the service, but it's one we'll all remember.

The next outdoor wedding I hoped would sail along smoothly was held in a beautiful backyard garden area especially designed for weddings. Dozens were held there each year. You would have thought they would have constructed bathroom facilities. But no such luck. Instead, they relied on a portable outhouse. That wouldn't have been so bad except it was located just twenty-five feet to the left of the pulpit area. If anyone had dared to use it during the service, their actions would have been quite apparent since it wasn't hidden well and any type of sound would carry. Fortunately no one chose to use that facility. It really wasn't very inviting.

As the service moved along, we did hear some strange noises. It seems we were in an area where people were allowed to own livestock—including mules. So not only did we have some beautifully taped music to set the tone and atmosphere for this ceremony, we also had the braying of mules. I always wondered if that came through on the recording of the service.

Just before we came to the point in the service where the other officiating minister was going to pray, I thought I smelled something burning. As everyone bowed their heads during the prayer, I didn't. I looked around, and right behind us were the candles. Since we were outside, the slight breeze that occasionally intensified was blowing the fronds of the ferns through the candle flame and the leaves were now singed. Realizing that no one was looking

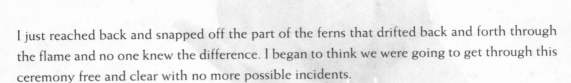

I just reached back and snapped off the part of the ferns that drifted back and forth through the flame and no one knew the difference. I began to think we were going to get through this ceremony free and clear with no more possible incidents.

Well, for the conclusion of the service the bride and groom had selected two white doves to release at this time. They were in a cage next to them. They each reached in and held one in their hands. As I looked out at the audience it dawned on me that everyone had the same question about these birds running through their minds: "Are they going to leave a deposit in the bride's and groom's hands or not?" The smirks on faces said this (later it was verified by some of the conversations I overheard during the reception). Fortunately the doves were released without incident and after circling two or three times they flew away. Finally we concluded the service. Several potential disasters were averted. However…there are many services in which what is remembered more than anything else is the disaster!

The following wedding mishaps border on being unbelievable, but they all happened:

A couple was married in a large facility designed just for weddings. They had hired a band for the reception dance. There was only one problem. The wrong band showed up!

In another wedding, the bride-to-be had decided to hold the rehearsal at her own home to help cut down on expenses. It was going to be a fairly large formal dinner. Caterers were going to oversee it, but she was still feeling a bit uptight. So to relax she spent the afternoon in her favorite relaxing activity—tending her flower and vegetable gardens. It had a wonderful calming effect on her, and by the time of the dinner she was relaxed. Everything went well, but it wasn't until the evening was over that she realized what had occurred. She was so relaxed she had forgotten to change out of her gardening overalls—she had worn them all evening. Everyone else either thought that's just the way she was, or they didn't want to be the one to mention anything—including her future husband!

This next wedding took place on a boat. The best man was assigned the task of keeping the ring. But when he took it out just to make sure everything was all right, the boat listed. The ring slipped from his fingers, bounced once, twice, and started to roll overboard. The best man leaped over the side of the boat, grabbed it in midair, and then hit the water. The guests loved it. So what if he was wet and when he walked water came out of his shoes? The ring and the ceremony were saved.

Clothes can be the source of some real surprises at weddings.

One groom forgot his good shoes and came down the aisle in his tennis shoes—it was better than being barefoot!

Another groom was so conscientious that he arrived at the church quite early to check on the arrangements. Then, just a half hour before the service was to begin, he went into the dressing room to put on his tux and realized he had left it at home—over an hour away. The organist noticed that the groom wasn't ready yet and asked if anything was wrong. He soon found out. Even though he was a bit larger, the organist offered his own tux. There was a partition around the organ so no one could see, so they made the switch right then and there. The groom went out to get in place and the organist began to play the "Wedding March"—in his underwear.

Wedding fiascoes can happen even to the best-known families.

President Woodrow Wilson's middle daughter, Jesse, was set to marry a young law student by the name of Frank. The couple followed the tradition of not seeing one another on the day of the wedding. Frank and the best man arrived at the White House. Unfortunately the front gate guard wasn't convinced that Frank was the groom, since neither he nor the best man had the necessary invitation with them. The time was getting short and the guard was adamant about not letting them in, but finally the captain of the guard arrived and allowed them to go up to the White House.

Why do couples even want to have birds as a part of their wedding? A couple scheduled their wedding at a large hotel's spacious ballroom. I'm not sure they even checked with the management about their romantic idea. They brought a flock of doves in cages so they could romantically "coo" through the ceremony until the couple said "I do," at which point the birds would be released to fly around as a tribute to the couple's love and devotion.

When they were released and the couple kissed, the audience was delighted at first. But their delight soon turned to chagrin as the doves kept not only flying around but laying claim to the clothing of the audience. They wouldn't leave the room as planned and sat on the chandeliers over many of the guests seated at the tables for dinner. Perhaps they should have provided their guests with umbrellas to fend off the birds' offerings. The moral is: What may sound romantic may turn into a mess if you don't think of the consequences.

Perhaps you heard about the mother who insisted that the chairs in the hotel's outdoor garden be bamboo, not upholstered. That was no problem. The switch was made. But not only were they bamboo, they were gold that clashed with the bride's colors of silver and white. That was no problem. The florist went out and purchased silver spray paint and said the chairs would be ready for the evening wedding. They were. That evening the bride and groom exchanged their vows while three hundred guests sat in the bamboo chairs. Everything went perfectly except for one small problem. The florist had neglected to use fast-drying paint. So every person received an unappreciated souvenir of the wedding. When they left their chairs they took with them a silver bamboo pattern imprinted on the back of their dresses and suits!

Have you ever been to a wedding celebrated by fireworks? Don't! You never know what might happen. One mother of the bride decided to celebrate her daughter's wedding by setting off fireworks on the lawn of her waterside home. The first rocket went screaming off into the sky and everyone was delighted. But something happened to the canister holding the other ten rockets. It tilted and shot the rockets every which way. One shot through the tent and one through the dining room window, which not only started a fire on the new carpet and on a friend's heirloom tablecloth but also on the wedding gifts sitting on top of it. The noise was so deafening it created some concern at a nearby naval station. Fortunately no one was hurt. A few months later the bride's mother received a gift from some friends. It was a specially made T-shirt that said "I Survived Carol and Dan's Wedding."

Accidents happen at weddings. Bubble machines at dances have created slippery floors so that the dancing guests created some new dance steps. Cakes have fallen off tables. At my daughter's wedding, my niece was eating cherry tomatoes when she bit into one and the insides exploded and shot out all over the back of a man's suit!

A young man went skiing three weeks before his wedding and broke his ankle. He returned home with a white plaster cast up to the middle of his calf. He felt terrible about it and thought he had ruined the wedding day and the big dance afterward. But his bride-to-be and her mother were very compassionate people with a great sense of humor. On the day of the wedding they had fake casts put on their legs and they all limped down the aisle. Everyone laughed and had a great time.

A little four-year-old boy was selected to be a ring bearer. He was a responsible, compliant child, so no one expected him not to follow the script. He started down the aisle. He walked several steps, stopped and faced one of the rows, made a ferocious face, and growled. He did this all the way down the aisle, and you can imagine the response. After the ceremony his chagrined parents asked him, "What in the world were you doing?" He replied, "I was doing what I was supposed to do. I was the ring bear!"

One bride was adamant about creating a Polynesian atmosphere for her wedding reception to be held in a country club. Eight men dressed in proper island attire walked in with the bride and groom carrying large tiki torches. Through this process two discoveries were quickly made: Tiki torches generate a lot of heat, and this heat will set off a sprinkler system. The sudden drenching everyone received was not in the program.

Today, every aspect of a wedding is captured on both video and audio. These recordings provide hours of delight. At one wedding a crew videotaped and recorded everything, including sounds they didn't expect. After the honeymoon the couple watched the video, and when they were cutting the cake it sounded as though there was a fountain in the room when there wasn't. Then they heard a sound they recognized—a flush. The audio man had forgotten to turn his microphone off when he went to the bathroom.

Hopefully your wedding will proceed without a hitch. On the other hand, it may not. What will make the difference? Attitude. Your attitude. Adjust, adapt, and enjoy. It's great practice for marriage.

VOWS FOR INSPIRATION

Groom: *(Name), you are the most beautiful woman I have ever seen. I love you in so many ways.*

I love the little girl in you who is so playful and enjoys each moment. I love the woman that you are, who is understanding and offers love and affection without conditions. (Name), you are the woman for me!

As your husband I commit to bringing God's truth and grace to our home. I will seek to act, rather than passively forsake, the role that God has given me.

As your lover I will not hide from you, even when I fear. I will make myself open and vulnerable to you, sharing my fears and hopes, both the unlovely and the lovely.

As your friend I will make time for us to listen and to talk. I will let go of tomorrow and enjoy the moment that we have, allowing the little boy in me to come out and play.

I pray that God will enable me to live out these promises, even as He already has, so that Jesus Christ might be glorified. I love you, (name)! I pray that you will find comfort in my arms all the rest of our days.

Bride: *(Name), I remember our first date…the openness, the honesty, the playfulness. Over the past year our relationship has grown even stronger in these areas, giving us the friendship we have today.*

I love sharing every area of my life with you because you are such a caring, sensitive, and loving man. You are always available to listen, support, and encourage me. I feel so safe and warm with you.

(Name), I know that your relationship with Jesus Christ has made you into the loving person you are. I promise to keep Christ first in my life as well, so that I may fully become the wife you deserve as we serve God together.

I desire to be available for you as well…to listen and support you in everything you do. I love you so much. I am proud to become your wife today, and I commit myself to you for the rest of my life.

The Ceremony

Do you remember the first wedding you attended? What were your impressions, your memories? How many weddings have you attended? Which was the most memorable? Why?

To assist you in thinking through what you would like in your ceremony, here are two wedding services with the words of the officiating ministers. As you read along, look for how the words speak about a Christian marriage. Consider the vows and what you might want to incorporate into your own ceremony.

THE WEDDING CEREMONY OF DAVID AND KATHERINE

Minister: David and Katherine, your wedding day has finally arrived: the day on which you make public vows of commitment. You may want to take a deep breath at this point. While it is an exciting occasion, it is also a day that can generate a great deal of nervousness. Fortunately, at least until now, everything has gone according to plan. Of course, wedding events do not always occur without mishaps. If we had time to interview those present this evening, I'm sure that we might hear some interesting stories of wedding-day problems—attendants who fainted, rings that were dropped, children who used the wedding as an opportunity to perfect their gymnastic skills. These types of misadventures do occur at weddings.

David, I ought to tell you that Katherine and I were once partially responsible for one of these wedding mishaps. Many years ago, Dad presided at a marriage where the groom's name was "Milfred." Several weeks before the wedding, Katherine and I began joking with Dad that he would have problems with the groom's name. We had no idea that the seeds of doubt we planted would blossom and bear fruit. Dad returned from the wedding and informed us that he had called the groom "Mildred" during the ceremony. Thankfully he did forgive us several years later!

While these wedding blunders are never part of our plan, they do provide a powerful reminder of the type of commitment you are making today. In the vows you will take, there are no conditional statements. Your commitment is not restricted to those times when all of life's puzzle pieces fall perfectly into place. No, the commitment you make today is a commitment to *endure*: a commitment that is not contingent on your circumstances. Even if today goes perfectly, there will be days in your marriage that won't. The obstacles that you may face come in a variety of shapes and sizes—difficult decisions, challenges in ministry, sickness, financial pressures. Katherine, it's the transmission that goes out on a day when your schedule has no margin for error. David, it's that church member who has the personality of a Brillo pad—every interaction seems to wear you down!

In these situations, there is always the danger that you unleash your frustration on your spouse. Consequently, these are the times that demand a commitment to endure. Of course, for us, *endurance* may not be a positive term—we tend to associate it with those tasks that involve hard work. At first glance, this commitment to endure may not seem inspiriting. However, in reality, it will have a liberating effect within your marriage. For it is in the context of this type of commitment that genuine intimacy develops and flourishes. Because of this commitment to endure, even in difficult circumstances, your marriage can be a place of refuge and encouragement. A useful tool that aids endurance is a healthy sense of humor. David, this is a particular strength of Katherine; she does have the ability to see the humorous side of disaster. She is the only person I know who has burst into laughter in the middle of an automobile accident, much to the surprise of the rest of the family.

As Christians, this commitment to endure ultimately originates in our confidence in God's character. It involves the recognition that God will not allow the heaviness of life's circumstances to outweigh the encouragement that He gives. It is built on the assurance that He can guide us through those difficult predicaments that we experience. What is the nature of the commitment that you are making? It is a *commitment to endure.*

Not only do your marriage vows involve a commitment to endure, they also entail a *commitment to forgive.* One of the ingredients of marital intimacy is vulnerability. Thus, when we are deeply intimate, we can also be deeply hurt. In the course of bringing two lives together, conflict and disagreement can emerge. Sometimes this tension results from minor actions and incidents. For instance, over the next few weeks you are going to learn a great deal about each other's daily habits; in the process you may realize that you do certain tasks differently. These differences, even if they are minor, can become a source of great irritation. As an example, do you squeeze the toothpaste from the end or from the middle? Do you meticulously roll the tube up so that every molecule of its contents has been removed, or do you throw it away long before reaching that point? For some, these are very significant questions. If this matter becomes a source of contention, Rose and I have discovered a simple solution—buy two tubes of toothpaste! Unfortunately, not all marital tension can be resolved this easily. Despite our best efforts, there can be moments in marriage when we hurt one another—a harsh word, an inconsiderate action. These types of situations demand that we learn to forgive.

But how can you truly forgive when you have been hurt? How can you forgive when your anger tells you that you should attack? Negatively, we can respond by denying our part or by simply mouthing halfhearted words of forgiveness. Of course, merely denying our hurt does not mean that it disappears. When left untreated, it may cultivate deep bitterness that eventually suffocates intimacy and closeness. No, genuine forgiveness does not begin with a denial of your emotions—it begins with open and honest communication. However, the goal is not to see how much emotional baggage you can unload; the goal is to speak the truth in love.

David and Katherine, that means expressing your hurt as well as expressing your love. It is only through the love that each of you has for the other that genuine forgiveness can take place. Love is the ointment that soothes the sting of damaged relationships. Not surprisingly in several passages, the apostle Paul's instructions about forgiveness are related to the importance of love. Love enables us to say "I forgive you" and really mean it. What is the nature of your commitment? It is a *commitment to forgive*.

There is one other aspect of your marital commitment that I would like to mention—a *commitment to grow*. As you begin your marriage, you are faced with a choice: You can allow your relationship to plateau at a level of peaceful coexistence, or you can commit yourselves to the process of growth and development. While a relationship that plateaus may be comfortable, it will rob you of an intimacy that thrives and flourishes. In a number of ways marriage provides remarkable opportunities for growth. First of all, marriage challenges you to grow in your expressions of affection. What are the best ways to say "I love you"? How can you communicate your compassion effectively? The more time you spend together, the more you will learn how to express your love in a way that is meaningful to your partner. For instance, David, I would suggest that a kitchen appliance might not be the most appropriate gift for Valentine's Day. On a number of occasions Rose has told me, "The day you give me a blender is the day I know the romance has gone!" Additionally, marriage challenges you to grow in your support of your spouse. For example, what are the ways you can affirm God's activity in the life of your partner? David, Katherine has always had remarkable people skills. Not only have these skills been evident in her social work, they have also been visible in her ministry activities. Make sure she has the opportunity for these gifts to develop and mature. Katherine, on a number of occasions you have mentioned your appreciation for David's integrity, his stability, and his character. Make sure that he is always aware of your appreciation and affirmation.

Just as marriage gives you the opportunity to grow in your affection and support, it will also give you the chance to grow in adaptability. To be successful, marriage requires give and take. You two are not exactly alike in your personalities, abilities, or interests; consequently, to develop meaningful intimacy, you will have to learn to adapt to each other. For example, for you, Katherine, this means that you will have to adjust to a new city, a new living environment, and a new role as a minister's wife. For you, David, this means that you will have to accept the fact that you will never have 50 percent of the closet space! My advice is this: Accept 35 percent and be grateful. There are no ways around it, marriage puts you in a situation that requires adaptability. One of my friends puts it this way: "Marriage is a commitment based on adjustment. If there is no commitment, it will fail: If there is no adjustment, it will be a living nightmare!" On the other hand, as you grow and adapt to one another, you will come to appreciate your differences and you will value the unique way God has equipped and shaped the character of your spouse.

So what is the nature of this commitment that you are making today? It is a *commitment to endure*, a *commitment to forgive*, and a *commitment to grow*.

David and Katherine, as you make this commitment, we want you to know that you are surrounded by family and friends who share your joy and happiness. As you begin this new adventure in marriage, we want to love you and encourage you. We are excited about what God desires to do in you and through you as husband and wife. As you make these vows of commitment, would you face each other, join hands, and repeat after me.

David, since you bear the responsibility for leadership in your home, you will begin.

David: I, David, offer myself completely to you, Katherine, to be your husband in marriage. I promise to love you with all my heart, to be true and faithful, to be kind and forgiving, and to be unselfish in this love. I promise to stand beside you always—in times of joy and in times of sorrow. I dedicate our marriage and home to the Lordship of Jesus Christ. I pledge myself, and all that I am, to you and you alone.

Katherine: I, Katherine, offer myself completely to you, David, to be your wife in marriage. I promise to love you with all my heart, to be true and faithful, to be kind and forgiving, and to be unselfish in this love. I promise to stand beside you always—in times of joy and in times of sorrow. I dedicate our marriage and home to the Lordship of Jesus Christ. I pledge myself, and all that I am, to you and you alone.

Exchange of Rings

Minister: The wedding ring has long been a symbol of covenant love. It represents a lifelong commitment of unswerving fidelity to each other. The unending circle serves as a daily reminder that there is no separation in your love for each other, so long as you both shall live. The open circle symbolizes the openness, the transparency, the trust that builds the strength and character of the other.

Andrew, would you hand me the ring that David has for Katherine?

David, as you take this ring and place it on Katherine's finger, please repeat after me.

David: With this ring, I commit all my love to you. As I love the Lord, so do I love you. I receive you as God's gift to me. As God empowers me, I will strive to lead our home under the Lordship of Jesus Christ. All that is mine is yours, until death and death alone should part us.

Minister: Rose, would you hand me the ring that Katherine has for David?

Katherine, as you take this ring and place it on David's finger, please repeat after me.

Katherine: With this ring, I commit all my love to you. As I love the Lord, so do I love you. I receive you as God's gift to me. As God enables me, I will seek to follow your leadership and support you in every challenge that life may bring. All that is mine is yours, until death and death alone should part us.

Pronouncement

Minister: Because you have pledged your faith in and love to each other, because you have sealed your covenant of love by the giving and receiving of rings, acting under the authority vested in me as a minister and looking to heaven for divine sanction, I now pronounce you husband and wife, in the presence of God and these assembled witnesses. Let no one ever separate what God himself has joined together.

THE WEDDING CELEBRATION OF MATTHEW AND SARAH

Minister: We are gathered here for a purpose both solemn and beautiful, both spiritual and earthly. We are going to witness the marriage of Matthew and Sarah, who have already promised themselves to each other in their hearts. In a moment of enormous significance in their lives—perhaps of more significance than anything they have done in a long time, or will ever do again, for from this moment their lives will grow differently—they will grow together. The way they see the world will be different. The way they relate to others will be different.

And the way they know and experience each other will be different.

They are not beginners in life. Each has had a certain lifetime already, with experiences of pleasure and pain, of joy and agony, of discovery and growth. But their times for such experiences are not over. Their union, celebrated here today and forged by the days and years that lie ahead, will lead to new pleasures and pains, new times of discovery and growth. Therefore, this is a mystical time in their journeys, a time of great spiritual possibility. And thus it is a time to be remembered and celebrated in the presence of God, where the burning of candles symbolizes the presence of the Holy.

Because it is a time of spirit and celebration, let us begin with prayer:

> *O God, who blesses all lives that are yielded to you in faith and sincerity, and without whom no life is ever blessed, we bow in your presence at the outset of this sacred experience. Give us all a sense of reverence for what we are about to do. Throughout human history, you have been especially close to persons whose lives were being brought into new relationships through marriage. Now, as Matthew and Sarah are joined before this altar, let us feel your closeness to them. Hallow the words we use and the air we breathe. Let the spirit and solemnity of this time never be lost to our memories. Through Him who loves us and sanctifies all our deeds. Amen.*

The Blessings of the Families

Minister: What Sarah and Matt do here affects the lives of others as profoundly as it affects their own lives. They have families whose relationships will be enlarged and with whom they now embark on a new adventure. We want to include the families and friends as well in our prayers and concern. So let us now pray for them.

> *O God, who is known in the encounter of person with person, family with family, and clan with clan, we magnify your name for being the One who binds all peoples together. In you, O Lord, shall all the nations of the world be blessed. Our days are as the grass that springs up today and tomorrow is cast into the oven, but your kingdom is forever. Teach us to find wisdom in our human limitations, and thereby to achieve more quickly the lessons of love and understanding.*

> *We pray for these two families being united today, that the ties of relationships being occasioned by this wedding will soon be transcended by a sense of genuine community among them. Let your blessing rest especially upon the children, for whom this may seem strange and not a little difficult. May they receive comfort and understanding in their hearts and soon grow into a sense of love and security in their new relationships. Grant that this ceremony and what is accomplished here may lead us all into ever deeper experiences of your grace. Through Jesus Christ our Lord. Amen.*

(Harp Solo)

The Preparation

Minister: Sarah, as you stand before God in the presence of all these people, do you do so with a contrite heart, asking God's forgiveness for all your sins and seeking God's leadership in the new life upon which you will now embark?

(I do.)

Matt, do you also, standing before God and in the presence of these people, come with a contrite heart, asking God's forgiveness for all your sins and seeking God's leadership in the new life upon which you will now embark?

(I do.)

The Blessing of the Rings

Minister: May I have the rings you intend to give each other? They are beautiful rings. Let us have a prayer of blessing for them.

> *Lord, these rings are simple, like your plan for our lives and happiness. They are unbroken in their roundness, like the ages in your sight. They are things of value, like your word given to us by the prophets and apostles of old. Let them become living reminders, we pray, of the simple, unbroken, and valuable love that Matthew and Sarah have for each other. Grant that nothing may complicate, break, or devalue that love. Teach them, whenever they look upon these symbols of affection, to remember this moment, this company of witnesses, this prayer, and your presence blessing their lives surrounding them with goodness and protecting them from evil. Amen.*

The Vows with the Exchange of Rings

Minister: Matt, as you place your ring on Sarah's finger and look into her eyes, please repeat after me the words of your sacred vow to her, taken before God and this company:

Matt: I, Matthew, take you, Sarah, as my dear and lawful wife. I commit myself to you as your faithful husband, to honor you as a person, to love you as my companion, and to cherish you as a child of God. I intend the love I have for you now to be only the beginning of the love I will come to have as the years go by. I look forward to sharing my life with you, whatever the future holds, and I will comfort you, confide in you, and journey with you from this day forth, whatever the conditions of our lives or of the world around us. So help me God.

Minister: Sarah, as you look into Matthew's eyes and place your ring on his finger, please repeat after me the words of your sacred vow to him.

Sarah: I, Sarah, take you, Matthew, as my dear and lawful husband. I commit myself to you as your faithful wife, to honor you as a person, to love you as my companion, and to cherish you as a child of God. I intend the love I have for you now to be only the beginning of the love I will come to have as the years go by. I look forward to sharing my life with you whatever the future holds, and I will comfort you, confide in you, and journey with you from this day forth, whatever the conditions of our lives or of the world around us. So help me God.

The Declaration of Union

Minister: This is a joyous moment. By the authority vested in me by the church of Jesus Christ, I now name you husband and wife, joined of God in the presence of all these witnesses. May God enrich you forever through the union you have made and bless your families with the benefits of each new relationship. You may kiss and embrace each other in the joy of what you have done.

The Prayer of Blessing

Minister: Now, having begun our celebration in the presence of the One whose holiness we adore, let us conclude by offering prayers of thanksgiving and petition. Sarah's fourth grade teacher, a longtime friend of the family, will offer this prayer of blessing:

> *We praise your loving mercy, O God, for the joy and excitement of this blessed occasion. It is you who have given us life and experience and you who have led us to this present moment. We acknowledge and bear you thanks for your everlasting care. Cast your mantle of grace and protection upon Sarah and Matt as they begin this new phase of their journey through life. Safeguard them from perils both seen and unseen. Make them trustworthy to each other and to all whose lives are affected by their marriage. Teach them day by day to love more gently, care more deeply, and share more generously. Let the sun always rise upon their goodwill and let it never set without it. Abide in their home as the One who imparts value to their relationships and meaning to all their efforts. Shelter them from the tragedies so common to human life, and support them that they may stand when visited by adversity. And bring them at last, when life's journey is complete, to rest and repose in our Savior Jesus Christ, to whom be glory forever and ever, world without end, and in whose dear name we pray.*

> *Our Father which art in heaven, hallowed be thy name. Thy kingdom come, thy will be done on earth as it is in heaven. Give us this day our daily bread. And forgive us our debts as we forgive our debtors. And lead us not into temptation, but deliver us from evil. For thine is the kingdom, and the power, and the glory forever. Amen.*

VOWS FOR INSPIRATION

Bride: *I love you, (name).*

I am so thankful for you. You are patient, caring, and trustworthy, and you always want the best for us. You are a gift from God, and your love for me truly demonstrates the love Christ has for us.

I believe in you, (name). I want to help make all your dreams come true. I have seen your love for God, and I promise to support your decisions and submit to your leadership knowing you always seek God's will. I promise to be faithful, and I will never leave you.

You are my best friend. I will pray for you daily, and I will always seek to grow closer to God. My desire is to be the woman you need me to be. I will make our home a place of rest, and I will always be there for you. I will listen to you and keep what I hear.

(Name), you are a wonderful, gifted man. You make me very happy. Laughter will always be in our home. You are the man I have always dreamed of and prayed for. I love you, (name), with all my heart.

Groom: *(Name), I love you.*

I am most fortunate to have found such a wonderful woman as a life partner. I happily anticipate having you as my wife and being your husband. Marriage comes with many responsibilities and even some surprises. I eagerly look ahead to them all so that we may grow together emotionally and spiritually.

I will be your spiritual leader: I will keep Christ at the center of our relationship so that we might have spirit-filled lives. As Paul wrote in Galatians 5:22-23, "But the fruit of the Spirit is love, joy, peace, patience, kindness, goodness, faithfulness, gentleness, and self-control," I dedicate myself to assuring our marriage will have an abundance of this fruit.

My arms will always be open to hold, comfort, and keep you safe as long as I am here on this earth.

(Name), I love you.

How to Create
Your Vows

The best Christian weddings reflect the bride's and groom's tastes, their relationship with one another, their relationship with Jesus Christ, and their own unique personalities. The key elements of a wedding ceremony, in their most common order, usually include:

- Opening words—given by the officiating minister (or ministers) and usually include a brief statement about the meaning, purpose, and value of love and marriage.
- Readings from the Bible, poems, or even an original writing from the couple—affirm and support the initial statement about love and marriage.
- A message from the minister to the couple—often addresses what a Christian marriage is and what the couple can expect.
- The question of intent—the couple is asked to promise those in attendance, the community, and God that they will create a stable, lasting marriage.
- The vows—promises and commitment the couple will make to one another. It is here that the originality of more and more couples is being expressed.
- Blessing and exchange of the rings—the minister blesses the rings before they are exchanged as symbols of the promises made in the vows.
- Blessing of the couple—the minister (or anyone else asked to do this) asks God for His support, blessing, and intervention on behalf of this couple for their marriage.
- Announcement or dedication—a summary and affirmation of what has just taken place.
- Closing words—usually a statement of hope by the minister for the future and an introduction to the audience of the new Mr. and Mrs. Bride and Groom.

Too many couples give little thought to *what is said* at each stage of a wedding. They simply follow an established script. Think about it. The words of your wedding, especially your vows, will be the focal point of your wedding. You want to create a ceremony that reflects your values, beliefs, and taste. Your pastor can help provide direction about the service, but this is *your* wedding, *your* marriage! What would *you* like said? What would you like *remembered* by your guests and by you?!

What would you like stated in the opening words? In Scripture readings? In prayers? What do you want your guests to hear that could impact their lives? The last chapters of this book, "Prayers and Scriptures for a Wedding Service" and "Quotes to Use for Your Wedding" (pages 137–200), are particularly helpful in this area. Share your ideas and hopes with your pastor. He or she may have other resources and selections from which to choose.

Take time to reflect on the weddings you've attended. What was memorable about each one? Was it what was worn? The decorations? What was said? The music? Does anything stand out? List below what comes to mind. Is there anything that you would like to incorporate into your service to make it memorable?

WRITING YOUR OWN VOWS

Wedding vows are the central theme of this chapter and book. Vows are usually reflective of three significant elements—your commitment to God, your commitment to marriage itself, and your commitment to each other. But where do you begin? What should be included in your vows? These are probably some of the questions that prompted you to search out this book.

Begin by thinking about your relationship with your future spouse. Use it to build your vows. The following questions are designed to help sort out some of the information you're looking for. Think about the questions and then write your responses. (Your partner should do this, too, only separately. Questions are repeated for the groom-to-be on page 76.) Don't read your partner's responses until you've completed your own.

For the Bride-to-Be

Where did you meet? Describe the setting, the time, the weather, etc.

What were your first impressions?

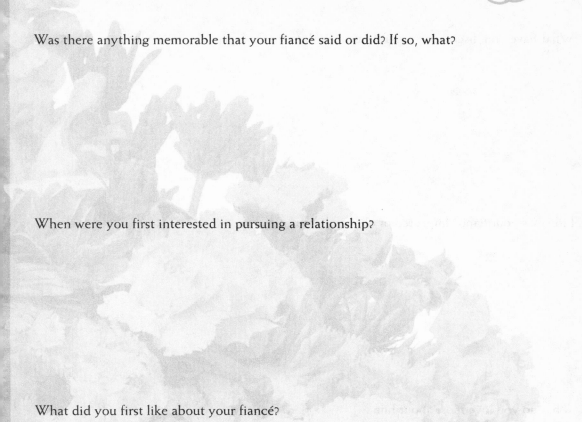

Was there anything memorable that your fiancé said or did? If so, what?

When were you first interested in pursuing a relationship?

What did you first like about your fiancé?

What have you discovered about him since then that is especially important to you?

How has your fiancé impacted or changed your life?

What do you love most about him?

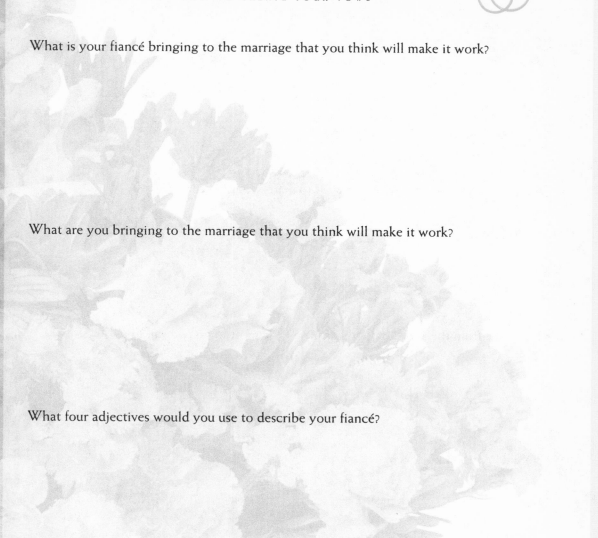

What is your fiancé bringing to the marriage that you think will make it work?

What are you bringing to the marriage that you think will make it work?

What four adjectives would you use to describe your fiancé?

What is the dream or vision you have for your life together?

What are at least six reasons why you want to marry your fiancé?

What passage from the Word of God has meant the most to you during this courtship?

Where did your first kiss occur?

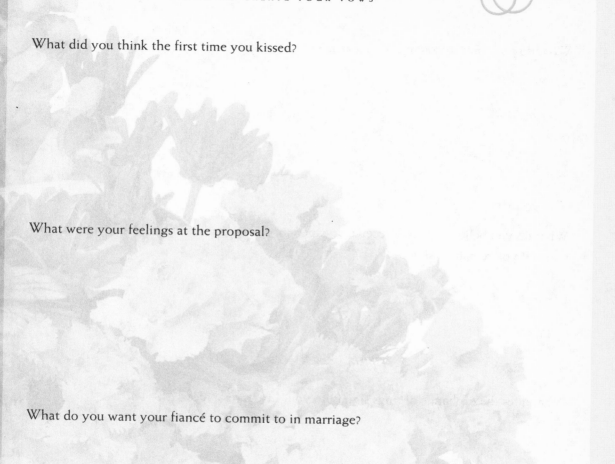

What did you think the first time you kissed?

What were your feelings at the proposal?

What do you want your fiancé to commit to in marriage?

What do you want to commit to in marriage?

What do you believe you will receive or experience out of marriage that you wouldn't experience if you remained single?

What does the exchange of rings signify to you? List several ideas.

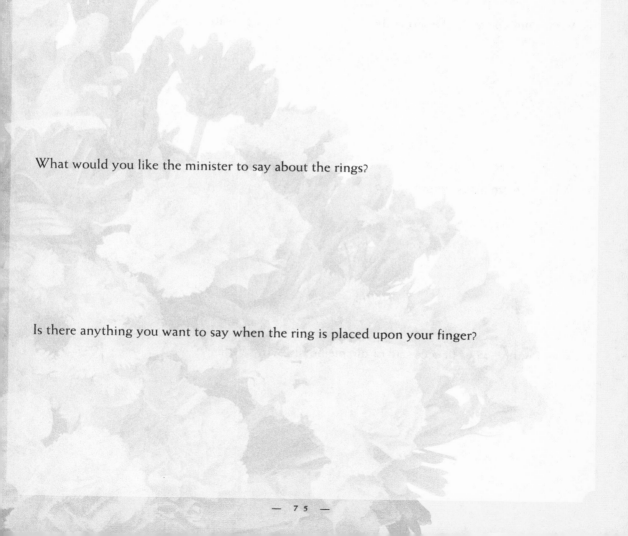

If you have already purchased your rings, what did that experience mean to you?

What would you like the minister to say about the rings?

Is there anything you want to say when the ring is placed upon your finger?

For the Groom-to-Be

Where did you meet? Describe the setting, the time, the weather, etc.

What were your first impressions?

Was anything your fiancée said or did memorable? If so, what?

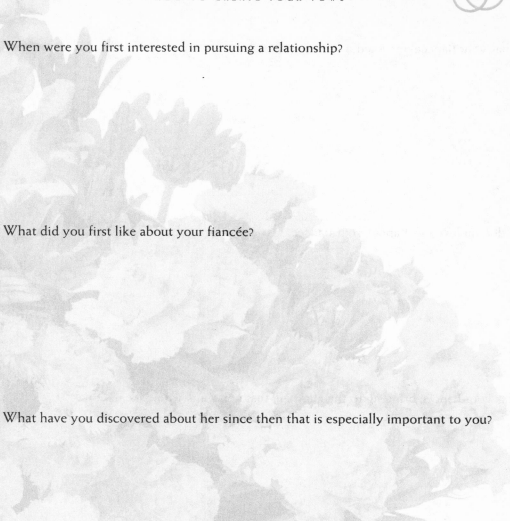

When were you first interested in pursuing a relationship?

What did you first like about your fiancée?

What have you discovered about her since then that is especially important to you?

How has your fiancée impacted or changed your life?

What do you love most about your fiancée?

What is your fiancée bringing to the marriage that you think will make it work?

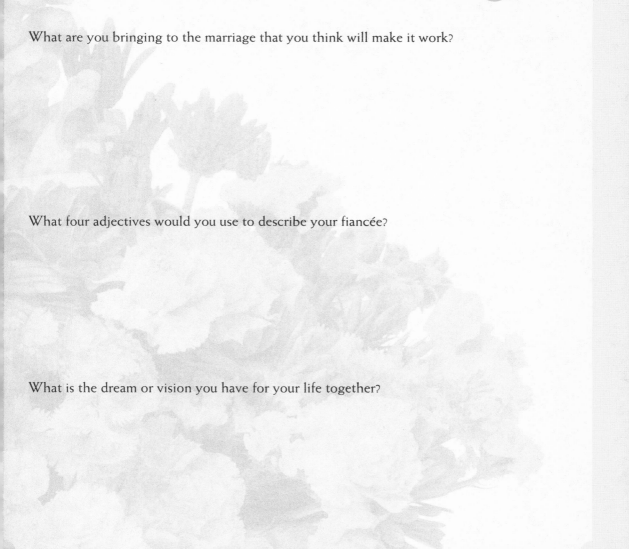

What are you bringing to the marriage that you think will make it work?

What four adjectives would you use to describe your fiancée?

What is the dream or vision you have for your life together?

What are at least six reasons why you want to marry your fiancée?

What passage from the Word of God has meant the most to you during this courtship?

Where did your first kiss occur?

What did you think the first time you kissed?

What were your feelings at the proposal?

What do you want your fiancée to commit to in marriage?

What do you want to commit to in marriage?

What do you believe you will receive or experience out of marriage that you wouldn't experience if you remained single?

What does the exchange of rings signify to you? List several ideas.

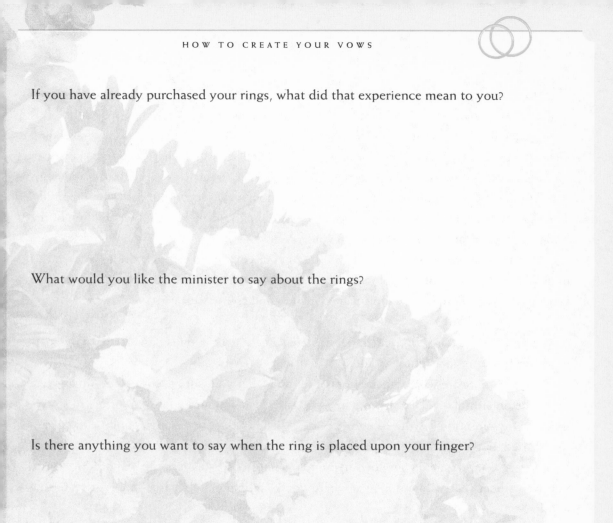

If you have already purchased your rings, what did that experience mean to you?

What would you like the minister to say about the rings?

Is there anything you want to say when the ring is placed upon your finger?

After both of you have completed your questions, read each other's responses. Take time to discuss thoroughly the answers. Out of these questions and the examples provided in this book you will find different themes and words you would like expressed in your own wedding vows. Remember, these are to represent you and your relationship. They need to be personal.

Some couples include their parents in the vows: The parents express their role and commitment in the couple's life and/or the bride and groom make a commitment to their parents. The next two chapters provide examples of vows to include others, including children of the bride and groom, and also reaffirmation vows.

When you are ready to start a rough draft of your vows, read through all the vows in this book. Circle the thoughts and phrases you like and begin to incorporate them into your own version. Perhaps these vows will trigger some new and creative ideas of your own.

As you create your vows, remember to state what you are promising to God, to the marriage itself, and to your future spouse.

Be positive: Share what you are hoping for and what you will do. Instead of phrases like "never be unfaithful" or "I'll never ignore you," say, "I *will* always be faithful" or "I will always give you my attention." Avoid using the phrase "I will try…." Too many couples end up saying, "I tried, but it just didn't happen."

Do you want to share your vows in monologue form, spoken by only one person? Or do you want them shared in a dialogue where you each express your lines alternately to one another?

VOWS FOR INSPIRATION

Groom: *I, (name), take you, (name of bride), to be my lawfully wedded wife. I promise before God and these witnesses and by the power of the Holy Spirit that I will rejoice and delight in you, becoming one with you as God has ordained. I will cherish and protect you. I will endeavor to be a godly, self-controlled man acting with kindness, consideration, patience, and humility in the heading of our household. I will endeavor to bring up any children we may have with love, fairness, and discipline, always teaching them according to God's holy Word. I will endeavor to love you as Christ loved the church, giving up my life daily in order to see you grow in every way that is pleasing to God, for as long as we both shall live.*

Bride: *I, (name), take you, (name of groom), to be my lawfully wedded husband. I promise before God and these witnesses and by the power of the Holy Spirit to love you always. I will leave my parents and become one with you. I will respect your headship even as Christ is head of the church. I will work with you as a united witness of the love of God. I will bring up any children we have with love, forgiveness, and discipline, always teaching them according to God's holy Word. I promise to love and cherish you and to prefer you above all others as long as we both shall live.*

Exchanging your vows is serious. It's not a time to share cute or funny statements to get a reaction from your guests. You'll probably have a number of one-liners or jokes come to mind as you create your vows. Share these with one another, but don't include them in the service, because it lessens the importance of what is taking place. Remember to keep this personal and meaningful to you. *This is what you are committing yourself to be and to do until death*. For some, that could be for another fifty to seventy-five years!

PROMISES TO MAKE AND KEEP

The following are promises that have been included in wedding vows. Perhaps there are some here you would like to incorporate into your own.

I promise:

   to live with you and love you forever

   to love you with a Biblical pattern of love, Eros, Philo, and Agape

   to be a source of joy to your life

   to meet all of your needs: emotionally, spiritually, and physically

   to be there when you need me and to respond in a way that meets your needs

   to laugh with you but never at you

   to bring out the best in you and always be your cheerleader

   to share and delight in your joy and to share your struggles during the down times

   to hear your tears, never try to fix you, and to wipe your tears with my hands

   to love you when you have wrinkles rather than smooth skin

   to love you with my mind and keep my mind focused on you

   to care for you in sickness of all kinds and in health

to care for you in the progress of your illness

to listen when you are worried, angry, or sad

to adventure with you into the unknown

to never take you for granted

to love your face and body as it ages

to be a person you can always depend on

to challenge you to be all that God wants you to be

to respect your wishes for your own children, your siblings, and your parents

to follow you wherever your life's vocation takes you

to pray for you and with you, and to initiate times of prayer

to be your spiritual leader

to forgive you quickly when I have been offended

to thank you for who you are as well as what you do

to love you, your father, and mother as well as any children God allows us to have through childbirth or adoption

to adventure into your life, to see it through your eyes, to hear it through your ears, to touch it through your fingertips

to select a passage of Scripture each week to live out in our marriage

to fulfill my responsibilities as given in Ephesians 5

to be faithful in seeking the Holy Spirit to direct my thoughts and words

to use the following Scriptures to guide my interaction with you

Most couples find they need to write at least a few drafts of their vows before they are ready. Pages are provided in the back of this book to record your vows as a keepsake.

After you have finished writing your vows, decide how you want to recite them during the ceremony. It's all right to have your pastor first say the vows phrase-by-phrase and you repeat them. It's also all right to read them aloud. You don't have to memorize your vows unless you want to, but even if you do, have them printed and available...just in case. There's a common malady that occurs at weddings called "brain blockage." It happens to the best of us.

Practice reciting your vows over and over. Share them in a loud, confident, and positive way. When you recite them at the wedding rehearsal, have someone stand at the back of the room or area to make sure you can be heard. Amplification equipment may be needed. Too many times guests leave a wedding without hearing what the bride and groom have said. Make yours a different experience. If you are going to have a wedding bulletin or program, consider printing your vows inside. Another option is to give a copy to guests as they leave.

To make your wedding commitment even more significant and meaningful, you could take these vows one step further by signing them during the ceremony. Have the vows printed in advance on a piece of parchment worthy of display (perhaps 11 x 14 inches). Then, for your wedding, have the paper placed nearby on a table or stand. After you recite the vows, the pastor can ask you to each step to sign and date the vows. We know that, for some reason, when people sign their name to a statement, agreement, or covenant, they seem to remember it better and follow through with their commitment.

Your vows could immediately be put in a glass frame and displayed at the reception for everyone to read. They could also be displayed in your home.

If your family and guests are asked during the wedding to make a commitment to pray for you, to be available for counsel, etc., this commitment could be on a parchment as well. The participants could be encouraged to read their commitment to you, and if they desire, sign their names to indicate their willingness to support you.

VOWS FOR INSPIRATION

Groom: *(Name), I love you and I am thrilled to take you as my wife today. I am thankful that God designed you with me in mind, and that I will not be complete without you.*

As God designed marriage and gave husband and wife separate and complementary responsibilities, I promise to be the head of our household. I promise to be the leader that you need, keeping our household focused on Christ.

Since love is in action, I promise to demonstrate my love to you in ways that you understand—showing you that I care. I promise to protect you, giving you a secure household in which you can share your innermost feelings. And I promise to listen and try to understand all of those feelings. Most of all, I desire to encourage you, helping you to become the woman that God wants you to be.

I have seen your love for God and your desire to serve Him, and I am truly blessed to have you love me as well. I am glad that you are my best friend, and I am honored to become your husband.

Bride: *(Name), I love you so much, and I am so glad that God has brought us together. I thank Him for you every day.*

I promise to be respectful of your leadership as the head of our family. Because you are a man of God, I am confident that you will be a loving spiritual leader, and I promise to support you in all of your decisions.

I will try to work toward a growing communication, keeping nothing from you. I will always listen to you, and when you confide in me, I promise to guard and keep what I hear.

I love you, (name). You are my best friend and I am proud and happy to become your wife today.

Vows to
Include Others

Wedding vows naturally focus on the bride and groom. However, there are occasions when the couple may want to include their parents in the vows. The parents may want to share a word of release to their children, affirm the new son- or daughter-in-law, or express the support the couple can expect from them. Likewise, some brides and grooms take part of the ceremony to respond to their partner's parents.

Including others in the vows is also becoming more and more popular in remarriages that involve children. Sample vows for blended families appear later in this chapter.

VOWS AND EXPRESSIONS FOR PARENTS TO SHARE

Parent: We stand here today as your parents feeling honored to be a part of this service. The two of us could not be any more delighted than we are with your decision to marry and spend your life together.

Every couple that marries comes with a bit of baggage. The two of us are a part of that baggage, but we hope we won't get in your way. Our role is to be on the sidelines cheering you on.

We commit to keeping our advice to ourselves (including any about your children if you choose to have any) unless you desire to ask for some. We will endeavor to keep it in the form of a suggestion that gives you the freedom to do with it as you desire.

We commit to making requests rather than demands, to be open with our feelings rather than allowing them to build up, and to give you the benefit of the doubt rather than think the worst.

We agree to discuss family gatherings with you rather than allowing unspoken expectations to guide us. Be patient with us as you create and carve out family traditions that may be different from ours.

We believe in both of you, in your decisions—even those that may take you far away from us—and in the impact you two can have upon the world for the sake of the kingdom of God.

Parent to future son-in-law: I love the way you relate to my daughter. You listen carefully to her and have a rare quality of being able to discern what's going on beneath the surface. As I have watched your relationship grow over the years, I have seen many times when you have responded to needs that she has at times not even been aware of herself. I love your teachable spirit that allows you to seek out and follow counsel and advice in order to strengthen the relationship between you and (name of bride). I love your willingness to listen to her, reassure her, and affirm her. Those are all very important to me because I love her, as you are demonstrating that you love her also.

Parent to future son-in-law: (Name of groom), you were not born to me as a son, but you have been born into my heart with all the fullness of love. I'm very proud and honored to call you my son-in-law. I love you.

You are a spiritually mature young man—one who consistently keeps your daily devotion time with the Lord, one who reads the Word daily and studies it to learn how God wants to apply it in your life. You pray about everything…you don't just move out in your own wisdom. You are not one to hide your light under a bushel, but you have a heart to bring others to the Lord. You know the importance of keeping in regular fellowship with other Christians. I see you keeping the Lord first in your life.

In the area of finances, I have seen you tithing, saving for the future, saving for expensive items, and budgeting for wise spending of your resources. In the area of nutrition and exercise, I see you practicing good habits.

I am very grateful that the Lord has chosen you to be (name of bride)'s husband. Likewise, I see that God has brought (name of bride) to you to be your helpmeet, who has been picked out by Him as perfectly suited and custom-tailored to be your wife. (Name of groom), I have confidence that you will be the spiritual leader of your family. I have already heard you and (name of bride) talk about raising children God's way.

I will continue to pray daily for God's continued guidance and blessing on you both and upon your marriage and family. May your marriage be a representation of the Lord's relationship to His church and thus be an example to others of God's agape love.

Parent to future daughter-in-law: I always knew this day would come. I have been praying for (name)'s lifetime partner since he was a little boy.

You seem to be God's answer to that prayer. I prayed God would prepare a godly young woman and draw that woman close to himself, save her, and create a hunger and thirst for the Word of God…that He would be preparing her to love, adore, and cherish (name of groom).

God knows and understands (name of groom). God knew who would be a good companion with whom to share his life, and I trust His choice.

I love your commitment to save yourselves for one another, and we know our Lord will bless your obedience.

Parent to future son-in-law: It is with great honor and pride that I present to you my beautiful daughter, (name of bride)—full of love, radiance, trust, hope, and dreams for a happy life.

(Name of groom), I have found you to be a very fine Christian gentleman—and worthy of her love. Your patience and understanding will be of infinite value. As (name of bride) grows and matures in your tender, compassionate love, her radiance will enrich, enhance, and enable your life. I am pleased to affirm many fine character qualities in you, and I am looking forward to you becoming my special son-in-law!

I have found you to be:

A man of your word—dependable

Decisive, committed, and consistent

Able to provide and protect

Intelligent and interesting

Thoughtful and loyal

Honest and willing to admit there's more than one way to do something

Goal-oriented and successful

A capable leader and organizer

Very talented and gifted

Friendly and people-oriented

A committed Christian

Perceptive with deep emotions

You were special from the moment we met!

VOWS TO THE PARENTS

Groom: As we stand here together, this is the day I've waited for, for years. I waited for a woman of quality with whom to share my life. You (bride) indeed are that woman. And who is it I can thank for this rare gift? First I give thanks to my Heavenly Father who is the giver of all the good and perfect gifts of life. But then I thank you, the mother of this beauty, for giving her life, for giving her charm, for helping her become the woman of character that she has become. I commit to you that I will always love, cherish, and protect her and never give you any concern for her safety and well-being. I will strive to meet her needs. And as she honors and respects you, I will do the same.

To you, the father of my bride, I thank you for being a loving father. You will always have a special place in her heart, and she will always be her daddy's girl. I pledge to you that I will now watch over her and honor her and love her forever.

Bride: To you, my husband, I thank God for you. I promise to love you today, tomorrow, and forever. I also promise to love and respect the two most special people in your life, your mother and father. Thank you [addressing parents] for helping to mold him into a strong, insightful, determined man. I promise you that I will learn to be the wife he has always wanted. My desire is to become as strong and stable for him as you have been over the years. Thank you for teaching him how to communicate, share his feelings, laugh, and look for the best in others. I believe he learned this from your example. You are not losing a son but hopefully gaining a daughter. Thank you for your act of releasing him from your home to me through the gift of your apron strings, cut from your favorite apron that you presented to me at the bridal shower. Thank you for guiding him to choose me.

VOWS FOR BLENDED FAMILIES

Groom: I stand here today, pledging myself, my love, and my possessions to you and also to (names of children). I commit myself to be a husband to you and a friend to your children. I respect your devotion to (names of children) and will never do anything to come between you and them or be a source of derisiveness in our home.

(Spoken to the children): I want both of you to know that I love and respect your mother and will always do so. I hope and desire to be an influence on your lives by listening to you, respecting your uniqueness and individuality, by teaching and suggesting and coaching, and by modeling. I pledge to you my goal to create a family atmosphere that is healthy and a place where you can grow to your fullest potential.

Minister to the children: As your mother and your father are entering into a new covenant relationship, your lives will be forever touched and influenced by their act of commitment. Your commitment will be needed to help create a new family that is healthy and fulfilling to each one of you. As your father and mother exchange their pledges and commitment in marriage, we ask from each one of you a promise, a commitment that you will make room in your heart and life for each new family member, whether it be a stepparent or sibling. Each of you is asked to be accepting, flexible, forgiving, loving, and willing to see life and events from the other person's perspective. Before God and all these witnesses we ask you to help this marriage and family by becoming the kind of person that God wants you to become. Will you accept this commitment challenge and your new relationship to (name of bride and/or groom)?

(The children respond, "We will.")

The following vows were made by a couple who each had two children from a previous marriage:

Bride: Susan and Tim, the three of us have shared many experiences and created many memories together over the past four years. We have learned to work and play together. We've been comfortable together, just the three of us, as well as Pepper, our dog. We've developed patterns and habits together; some of which are daily routine. Now we're about to change some of our patterns and routines. We've talked about this before, but today is the day for us to let the world know our intentions. Our big step is to join our family with Fred and his two children.

Mary and Tess, I love your father so very much, and I love you very much as well. Susan and Tim also want you as members of this big family. It will be an adventure, and not always easy, but worth every effort and moment.

Groom: This is a big step for me, for us. Mary and Tess have asked me for years if I would marry. I kept saying no, but Renee, you changed my mind. I saw in you the wife I always wanted and the companion for my girls. Mary and Tess have been marking off the days for weeks, and I'm delighted we've all shared the experience of rearranging, redecorating, and totally changing a single man's big house to make it reflect all of us. We, all of us, will need to rely upon our commitment to one another to make it through the difficult times of adjusting to one another. We are committed to working toward bringing together two families of three and creating one family of six. We, too, vow this is an adventure.

These vows were made at a wedding in which the groom had four children:

Groom to bride: Nancy, my beloved, I remember the first time we met. It was for lunch at the Bagel Café. I knew that there was something special about you, and I couldn't wait for our next date…and the next one after that…and the next one after that. I was falling deeply in love with you. And now our special day has arrived. Nancy, I promise before God and these witnesses to commit to you my fidelity, my honor, and my trust. I promise to protect you and keep you safe. And most of all, Nancy, with God's help I promise to love you as Christ loved the church. To hold you and cherish you all of our days.

Bride to groom: Bob, my beloved, I've waited a long time for this day. I dreamed of my wedding day, but I never dreamed I could be so deeply in love as I am with you.

Bob, I do pledge before God, our families, and dear friends to take you—to respect, to assist, and to cherish you as long as we both shall live. I do vow by all that I hold sacred to love you as husband and friend, to walk beside you in life with the blessings of our Lord. To you I promise my fidelity and my trust, my laughter and my tears. I promise you my strength, my comfort, and my warmth. I shall love you in honesty and joy, and this I offer in the sacred name of Jesus Christ.

Bride to groom and his children: My beloved, as I promise to love and cherish you as husband and friend, so do I promise to love, teach, protect, and enjoy these children as my own. I will not attempt to replace anyone, but to be a friend and make my place in their hearts.

To Tara: I promise to be an encourager. I hope to be a big sister, sometimes a mom if you need me to be, someone who will believe in you.

To Bobby: I promise to always have food in the house, to support your life and your love of life, to be a listening ear if ever you need one.

To Jessica: I promise to appreciate your beautiful individuality, to take you on shopping

trips, and to cherish your tender heart.

To Jimmy: I promise to always listen, to try to figure out some computer games, and to encourage you in the talents God has given you.

To you all: I vow my trust and my joy that we may be together, to laugh, to cry, and to celebrate our individuality. On this day when I marry your father, I also join to you, and I promise to love and support you as my own.

If the bride and groom have adult children, they may want to create a statement together that one of them will read as part of the ceremony:

Adult child: The five of us have met together, and we are of one mind and thought concerning your coming together in marriage. We couldn't be more delighted. We love you very much and are happy for your newfound happiness. You have always been there for us with your love and support and we promise that we will always be there for you with our love and support. We will pray for you and be available if and when you need us in sickness and health. We thank God for your godly example and pray that our children will be influenced by you as we were. We pray that your lives together will be more fulfilled and rich together than alone.

VOWS FOR INSPIRATION

Groom: *When I was very young, I committed my whole heart and life to Jesus Christ. It was and is my desire and commitment to live a holy life that is pleasing to God. My passion is to know God and to know Him more fully and to grow in His grace and wisdom. To seek His face and know His voice. It is in that commitment that I commit my life to you. I promise to lead our family as a husband and father whose heart's desire is to be Christlike. To be humble, meek, gentle, strong, forgiving, patient, and loving. It is my desire to do all that I can that (names of bride's children) would see Christ in me. To love them as my very own. To be a leader they can follow.*

I will be there for you to encourage you, listen, protect, comfort, and be faithful to you forever. I want to walk side by side with God in valuing you as the gift that you are. I want to do all that I can to help you become all that God wants you to be. To love you as Christ loved the church.

(Name of bride), you are my treasure, my gift from God. You are my best friend, my love. I am so thankful that God has brought you into my life. I look forward to a lifetime of having you by my side, serving God together. I love you with all my heart.

Bride: *As I stand here today, I am humbled by all that God has given to me in you. God knew the deep longing in my heart long ago for a man of godliness, a man of gentle strength and strong character, a man of loyalty and devotion. He has given all of that to me in you and so very much more. You have loved me with all the sweetest love. And you have loved* my boys as you would your own. You allowed each of us time to know the character of your heart, to see the integrity in your life, and to trust the love you have for each of us. What an incredible blessing you have been.

(Name of groom), it is my prayer that I will be found a woman who treasures all that God has given. I will continually seek to grow in my relationship with our Lord, which will enable me to be the woman I need to be for you. And I will encourage you to do the same. I will love you, I will honor you. I will respect you, and I will teach our children to do the same. I will come alongside you to be your helper and to be a complement to your life. I will care for you when you're well and when you're not. I will be faithful to you every day of my life. I will be your most trusted friend and companion. I will also gently challenge you at times when you need that. I promise to pray for you continually, and to share in your love and commitment to God. I know that at times I will disappoint you. I wish I could promise you that I won't. But I will always try to be my best for you, to listen when I'm wrong, to be open to change when that's needed, to compromise.

I look forward with excitement for all that God has planned for us. I am thrilled to be spending the rest of my life with you. I love you with all my heart.

Reaffirmation of
Your Vows

More and more couples are having reaffirmation ceremonies. It's a positive step for a couple, whether the motivation stems from having experienced difficult times and overcoming the adversity to creating a ceremony signifying, "We've made it for forty years and we just want to renew the step we took years ago."

Someone said that if the wedding ceremony is the celebration of falling in love and starting a marriage, a reaffirmation ceremony could be considered the celebration of still being in love and staying married.

I've participated in several of these events. One was the ceremony of a close friend and his wife. They married in high school, had a baby right away, and at first lived in a converted chicken coop while working on an egg farm. They met the Lord a few years later and their lives changed. They are survivors. They wanted to declare their lasting commitment to each other and to Jesus Christ. It was a special time, not just for them, but for everyone there.

Another couple had been separated for almost two years. The husband became involved with someone else during that time, but fortunately that relationship dissolved. A few months later he became a Christian in a very dramatic life-changing way. After he and his wife reunited they had a ceremony in their backyard, created new vows, and recited them. Not only that, they shared their personal journey with everyone there and gave an invitation to accept the Lord. It was a very moving and powerful time.

Why do couples renew their vows? It's not to meet any of society's standards or legal requirements or religious guidelines. It's quite simple—they want to.

It's a chance to redefine their marriage, rededicate themselves, celebrate what they've accomplished and look ahead to what they have before them. Though that personal statement may include many of the elements of a first-time wedding, the emphasis is very much on their own relationship and commitment, on all the unique and personal things that have made their marriage endure.

In reaffirmation all the forms and customs of a wedding take on a special meaning. While many first weddings are events involving the families of the bride and groom, a reaffirmation celebrates the family you've created together. A reaffirmation is given by you, not by your parents; you are the hosts, and your parents are honored guests who share your day with you. A reaffirmation is also a chance to include your children in your marriage in a very meaningful way. It's their chance to do something for you through their presence and participation in your event. A reaffirmation can be very much a reflection of your family history—the roots of your marriage, your experiences through the years, your hopes for the future. [1]

What is reaffirmation? In a sense it's the opposite of a divorce decree. It's an act of rejoicing over the fact that you've been able to make marriage work, to make it fulfilling, to weather the storms, and to fully possess your marriage. You're not discontinuing the adventure. Reaffirmation is the outward public demonstration of renewing your commitment to one another. It's outward because it takes daily effort and commitment for your marriage to be all you want it to be.

Reaffirmation is once again making a choice—a new choice. The reasons for this act are probably much different from the reasons you originally wanted to marry your spouse. Instead of basing it upon a hope of future dreams fulfilled, it is an act based upon a history of what has occurred as well as the hope for the future. One marriage therapist described reaffirmation this way:

Reaffirmation is, first of all, an exploration, a redefinition of where you are as a couple. It can involve a questioning of the whole marital relationship. Each partner may ask, "Am I getting what I want or need out of this relationship? What if my spouse gets really sick and becomes bedridden or infirm—how will I feel about taking care of him or her? Will I be overwhelmed by resentment and bitterness? Granted that everyone has some resentment under those circumstances, would I be able to live with my resentment and still remain a person who cares for his or her spouse? Have we as a couple continued to develop interests in common, or has our life together become boring and repetitive? Do we stimulate each other intellectually? And how important is that aspect of our lives? The years of my life are precious ones. Do I trust my mate enough to risk spending them with him or her?"

Reaffirmation challenges me to examine myself, as well. "Where am I at this point in my life? Where do I want to go? Has my relationship enabled me to grow sufficiently, or have I found it to be thwarting and confining? When we first met, we married for very specific reasons. Are those reasons still valid? Have they changed? If I were to marry again now, would I select the same mate?"

Deciding to renew your vows can involve some soul-searching questions. It takes people who have a good sense of who they are and who have sufficient self-esteem to be able to take a long, hard, honest look at themselves and their relationship. But questions needn't be frightening. They have the potential for leading you to a place that's deeper, richer, more profound.[2]

How can an affirmation service be a memorable experience, not only for the couple, but for those in attendance? It's true this service is for the couple and their marriage, but what an opportunity to minister to others at the same time.

- If you videotaped your wedding, select portions of it to play at the beginning of this time or throughout the service. Still pictures can also be made into a sort of video scrapbook.

- If you have videos of the two of you over the length of your marriage, show brief segments and then describe what was going on in your life at that time. If this is your twenty-fifth anniversary, show pictures or film from five-year intervals. If it's a fiftieth anniversary, select photos at ten-year intervals.

- One or both of you could share with those in attendance what you have learned during your marriage. This could be done live or even videotaped beforehand.

- You may want to share significant quotes from books that you've read on marriage.

- Share with your guests the various answers to prayer that you've experienced over the years.

- You may want to reaffirm your vows in a private ceremony with no one in attendance. You could have it videotaped and then send copies to significant people in your life.

- Let those in attendance know what you'll need from them for the future enhancement of your marriage. Give people the opportunity to share with you and the group words of wisdom or encouragement or a blessing.

- If your parents are living, there may be some way you might want to include them in this time.

A reaffirmation ceremony is your celebration, so plan whatever you would like. (After all, you will likely be footing the bill.) To create your renewal vows, the questions, sample vows, and poems that appear later in this chapter will be particularly helpful, but almost any of the vows, phrases, quotes, and Scripture readings in this book can be used or adapted for a reaffirmation ceremony.

If you have children, not only plan to have them at the ceremony, but depending on their ages, you could involve them in some way, from preparations to helping at the event itself. Some senior couples have involved grandchildren as well as great-grandchildren. Your parents as well as any relatives who are close to you would be invited. But this is not an occasion in which you have to invite relatives—or anyone for that matter—out of a sense of obligation.

Remember, this is a couple affair. As much as possible, involving both husband and wife to the same extent will benefit the couple. This event needs to represent the thoughts, feelings, needs, and desires of both husband and wife.

The friends you invite may be some of those who came to your wedding as well as new ones. Again, obligation is not a factor but more your desire of whom you would like to be a part of this occasion.

What should your invitation state? Again, it's up to you. It can be serious or funny, formal or casual. Here are some possibilities:

> *Mr. and Mrs. Ken Jones request the honor of your presence*
> *at the reaffirmation of their original wedding vows.*
>
> *Saturday, July seventh, two thousand and one*
> *At one o'clock*
> *At Hollywood Presbyterian Church*
> *Carlos and Gower, Hollywood, California*
>
> *R.S.V.P. by July first, two thousand and one*

If children are involved in the reaffirmation ceremony, the first line of the invitation might be changed to: "The Jones family requests the pleasure of your company to celebrate the reaffirmation of the wedding vows of Ken and Nancy Jones."

The following note demonstrates a more personal style:

> *It has been twenty-five years, a quarter of a century, since the two of us were united at Southwest Church. It has been an exciting, event-filled journey for both of us. By the grace of God we've reached our first milestone and anticipate at least another twenty-five years.*
>
> *Therefore we are once again going to say our vows to one another. It would mean so much to us if you could join us for this time of commitment, celebration, and feasting.*
>
> *We look forward to hearing from you.*
>
> *(Please, no gifts. Your presence will be a sufficient source of lasting joy.)*

The following style is even less formal:

Come and join us at the ranch for a western-style reaffirmation ceremony.

It's been twenty years and they have been good ones. Instead of walking down the aisle we'll be riding down the trail on our horses, and Pastor Bob, who performed our ceremony twenty years ago, has agreed to lead this ceremony (no horse for him—he's standing on the buckboard).

Our theme is western, so please dress appropriately. Even a western hat or red handkerchief will suffice.

In the tradition of western get-togethers, food is a big part of this gathering, so please bring a western-type dish for ten people to add to everyone's enjoyment. Please park outside the gate and catch a ride on the horse-drawn wagon up to the house.

A combination formal-humorous invitation could be like the following:

> *We, the children of Ken and Marcia Britton, wish to invite you to the recitation and reaffirmation of our parents' wedding vows and fortieth anniversary celebration.*
>
> *This will be held in their home at*
>
> *2000 Prospect Avenue at 2:00 p.m., January 27, 2002*
>
> *Since they were high school sweethearts and survived the chaos of the fifties and sixties, the theme for the dinner and dance will be the fifties and sixties. Please dress to reflect this cultural anomaly.*
>
> *No gifts of a value less than $1,000 will be accepted. And we do not accept credit cards.*

CREATING RENEWAL VOWS

How do you fashion vows of reaffirmation? This is a time of realistic recommitment. It's also a time to reflect back over the history of your marriage and perhaps incorporate some of these experiences into the vows. Your vows and sharing may become lengthy. For some, it's easy to speak off-the-cuff and remember everything you want to say. For most, it's not. For some, memorizing a lengthy selection is quite easy, but for others it's a pressurized chore. There's nothing wrong with reading what you have to say, recording it, and then playing the tape or even making a video beforehand using cue cards. Make this day as relaxed and as comfortable as you can. The following are some topics you may want to consider using to enrich your vows:

When or where you met
Your first impressions
What drew you to this person
When you first realized you were in love
Your first kiss
Your favorite places
Reasons why you married this person
Reasons why you're glad you married this person
Dreams for marriage you had that were realized
Surprises you've experienced in your marriage
Special times when you were dating and during marriage
Special anniversaries and valentines
A time when you especially experienced God's presence together

Reaffirming vows is an opportunity to remember why you are together and why you ever got together in the first place. It's a remembering of your first love responses. When you reaffirm your vows you are declaring that you have discovered the meaning of this Scripture passage:

> *This love of which I speak is slow to lose patience—it looks for a way of being con-*

structive. It is not possessive: it is neither anxious to impress nor does it cherish inflated ideas of its own importance.

Love has good manners and does not pursue selfish advantage. It is not touchy. It does not keep account of evil or glad over the wickedness of other people. On the contrary, it is glad with all good men when Truth prevails.

Love knows no limit to its endurance, no end to its trust, no fading of its hope; it can outlast anything. . . .

In this life we have three great lasting qualities—faith, hope and love. But the greatest of them is love (1 Corinthians 13:4-8, 13, J. B. Phillips translation).

Consider these thoughts about love:

Love gives us courage to be our best. When we doubt our lovability we are always less. Love inspires us to realize our potential. With love, a dependent person can become independent, a controlling person can become free, and a competitive person can learn to nurture others.

Our partner's love is a reminder that we are lovable even when we are not our best, but it cannot replace self-love.

Love is a support, but although it is freely given it is not a permanent loan. Love is a flow *of feeling. To keep it moving in both directions, the partners have to be worthy of the love bestowed on them.*

The most satisfying part of loving another person is seeing your love make a change for the better.

In times of adversity, remember your love.

When there is a choice, come from love.

Coming from love is not avoiding pain, but insisting on healing.

Coming from love is allowing others to be one with their sadness so they can mourn and clear the way to feel joy again.

Coming from love is being your best in the presence of others.

The love that flows through you is only partly a response to the people you love.

If you are in doubt, come from love and you will understand.

If you are in pain, come from love and you will grow.

If you are forsaken, come from love and you will find happiness again.

Love means to care about the feelings of another as if they were your own.

Love is the acceptance that comes with knowing all of a person's faults and not rejecting the other for what you discover, but rather living in expectation of good. The great peace of love is that there are no surprises you can discover that will cause you not to love the other. The love that lasts is based on the partners' acceptance of themselves as they truly are.

Love is trust. You trust that good abides in you and that you are worthy of being loved. You trust that you are being treated directly and fairly and you trust that your partner feels the same way.

This is the rule of love, that love is open and love is free.

This is the rhyme of love, that love is answered and accommodated, that crowded schedules change and opportunities for togetherness are created out of pressure and chaos, that distances are bridged, absences endured, and joining celebrated.

Love has priority. Love is first. Love is now. Love is best. Love is also next and last.

This is the rhythm of love. It is an inner motion seeking to dance among the stars.

The perspective of love is ever closer and larger, warmer and freer. It is open and giving, expanding and encompassing. It is a generosity of feeling because it recognizes the sameness of feelings between you. It is a passion among equals or it is nothing at all.

The dance of love is a quickening of heart, a belief in the impossible because it is suddenly real.

Love is honesty made visible.

Love is giving made acceptable.

Love helps the needy grow from envy to self-acceptance, from possessiveness to self-confidence, and from jealousy to trust in ourselves.

We need love the way we need air. We need love the way we need food. We need love the way we need love.

When you are in a relationship that nurtures and accepts you, you stop striving for the symbolic rewards that comfort a troubled soul. You feel peace because you have the thing you need. A house is empty without love, but a soul is empty if it does not love its oneness. You cannot love another person unless you can abide your own singularity, your aloneness, your being with yourself.

A life without love of self is a lonely life.

A life without love of another is an unreflected life.

Love is openness and wonder. Love is relief, spawned of sharing intimacies and self-doubt with childish candor. Love is simple and love is easy, when love is easy.[3]

SAMPLE RENEWAL VOWS

Husband: I am standing here before you, much calmer and more aware of what I am doing than I was the day we joined together. You have become my best friend, my favorite person, my lover, my partner in parenting. I hold you tighter now than ever before because I am so much more aware of what I would lose if you were not with me. As we renew our vows, I am much more aware of what I am saying and doing than I was many years ago. I am glad to do this over again. What you and I have been through together God has used to shape us into who He wants us to become. There have been difficult times, differences, challenges, learning to cook and eat new dishes, adjusting to our different families—none of these experiences would I ever trade because we were together in all of them.

When I was weak, you were strong. When I had a need, you were there. You encouraged me and believed in me. I commit myself heart and mind to you and you can count on me for the rest of our days. I loved you first as a girlfriend, then a fiancée, next a bride, and now as my lifelong companion. I thank God for you and will pray for you each day.

Wife: I stand here today holding your hands tightly. I didn't want you to ever get away the first time I saw you and I still don't. That's why I am recommitting myself to you today and forever. You have changed as I have changed. You are more confident, still thoughtful, and choose your words carefully. Even though your words are not as abundant as mine, I delight in hearing every one and am willing to wait for them. We both have changed physically, a bit of gray dots the side of your head, and I love the color. Wrinkles are beginning and will become more pro- nounced. If you can stand mine, I know I will love yours. Thank you for your commitment over the years, which I saw in changing diapers, tolerating my new recipes, asking first if I was all right when you saw the dented fender, and helping me when I cried rather than trying to fix me. Thank you for believing in me. I look forward to being by your side, being in your bed, being in the boat on the lake, and helping you gather the money we'll need for our children's weddings and our grandchildren.

I commit myself to always being your bride, in sickness or in health, when finances are abundant or when the bills have stacked up. I will continue to learn who you are as you continue to learn who I am. And I will continue to bring you before our Lord and Savior Jesus each day of our life.

The following two poems may help you to create your own thoughts:

On the Eve of Their Golden Wedding Day
John C. Bonser

"Our Golden Wedding Day draws near," the husband said.
The elderly woman, smiling, raised her head,
"Will you write me a poem as you used to do?
That's the gift I'd like most from you!"

The old man, agreeing, limped from the room,
Went out on the porch in the twilight's gloom,
Leaned on the railing and reminisced:
"Often we sat here, shared hopes, and kissed."

"Dear Lord, how the years have hurried by—
Those memories of youth make an old man sigh!
Now we grow weary and bent and gray,
What clever words can I possibly say

"To show that I love her just as much
As I did when her cheeks were soft to my touch,
When her eyes were bright and her lips were warm
And we happily walked with her hand on my arm!"

So the husband stood while the evening breeze
Echoed his sigh through the nearby trees
Till the joys they had shared in days long past
Merged into thoughts he could voice at last,

And he went inside and got paper and pen;
Sat down at the kitchen table and then
Carefully wrote what his wife had desired;
A gift as "golden" as a love inspired.

"Sweetheart, dear wife, my closest friend,
With you my days begin and end.
Though time has stolen strength and youth,
It cannot change this shining truth:

Our love has lasted all these years
While hardships came and sorrow's tears.
We've met each test and gotten by,
And I will love you till I die!
We are not rich in worldly wealth
But we own nothing gained by stealth,
And you remain my greatest treasure,
My source of pride and quiet pleasure.
I wish you all the happiness
With which two loving hearts are blessed;
You were, and are, my choice for life,
My girl, my lady, my sweet wife!"

The poem finished, the husband arose,
Went into the room where his good wife dozed
And tenderly kissing her nodding head,
"Wake up, 'sleeping beauty,' and come to bed!"[4]

The Worn Wedding-Ring
William Cox Bennett

Your wedding-ring wears thin, dear wife, ah, summers not a few,
Since I put it on your finger first, have passed o'er me and you;

And love, what changes we have seen, what cares and pleasures, too—
Since you became my own dear wife, when this old ring was new!

O, blessings on that happy day, the happiest of my life,
When, thanks to God, your low, sweet, "Yes" made you my loving wife!
Your heart will say the same, I know; that day's as dear to you—
That day that made me yours, dear wife, when this old ring was new.

How well do I remember now your young sweet face that day!
How fair you were, how dear you were, my tongue could hardly say;
Nor how I doted on you; O, how proud I was of you!
But did I love you more than now, when this old ring was new?

No—no! No fairer were you then than at this hour to me;
And, dear as life to me this day, how could you dearer be?
As sweet your face might be that day as now it is, 'tis true;
But did I know your heart as well when this old ring was new?

O partner of my gladness, wife, what care, what grief is there
For me you would not bravely face, with me you would not share?
O, what a weary want had every day if wanting you,
Wanting the love that God made mine when this old ring was new!

Yours bring fresh links to bind us, wife—young voices that are here;
Young faces round our fire make our mother's yet more dear;
Young loving hearts your care each day makes yet more like to you,
More like the loving heart made mine when this old ring was new.

And blessed be God! All he has given are with us yet; around
Our table every precious life lent to us still found.
Though cares we've known, with hopeful hearts the worst we've struggled through;
Blessed be his name for all his love since this old ring was new!

The past is dear, its sweetness still our memories treasure yet;
The griefs we've borne, together borne, we would not now forget.
Whatever, wife, the future brings, heart unto heart still true,
We'll share as we have shared all else since this old ring was new.

And if God spare us 'mongst our sons and daughters to grow old,
We know his goodness will not let your heart or mine grow cold.
Your aged eyes will see in mine all they've still shown to you,
And mine in yours all they have seen since this old ring was new.

And O, when death shall come at last to bid me to my rest,
May I die looking in those eyes, and resting on that breast;
O, may my parting gaze be blessed with the dear sight of you,
Of those fond eyes—fond as they were when this old ring was new![5]

VOWS FOR INSPIRATION

Husband: *I recommit to sharing myself and my life with you.*

I will be your friend and your love—a source of strength and safety—someone who dreams with you.

I promise to love you unconditionally, and realize that this involves sacrifice as well as great rewards.

I will continue to stand with you whatever happens—in laughter and in tears, in the woods and in the city, now and forever.

And yet I will grant you space to be yourself, knowing that we are tied together and trusting that nothing can come between us.

You are an amazing person, and I respect and accept all of who you are.

Wife: *I recommit to sharing all of who I am with all of who you are.*

I will continue to be your friend and your lover, your teammate and your lifelong companion.

I promise to care about you—to cherish your uniqueness, to encourage your process of becoming, and to respect you always.

I will continue to stand with you—in laughter and in tears, in agreement and in conflict, in the woods and in the city, knowing that whatever we are together will be beautiful.

I promise to love you in the way that befits a precious child of the Creator.

Variations in the Wedding Service

These days we enjoy greater freedom in making a wedding ceremony unique and special. The following ideas can be used to incorporate creative, personalized elements into your own service or help you create new expressions of your relationship with each other and with Christ.

A friend of mine and his wife had a large Bible that had been in the family from the previous century. Every marriage, birth, and death in the family was recorded in this Bible, so it carried rich historical significance for the entire family. When their son got married, the Bible was displayed in a prominent spot near the bride and groom on the platform where the wedding ceremony took place. After the minister pronounced them husband and wife, the couple went forward and added their names to the Bible. At the reception the Bible was displayed so guests could view all the names and become better acquainted with the family's history.

A number of years ago I had the privilege of doing the premarital counseling for a very special couple. I had known the groom for a number of years and had been blessed by his singing ministry, which featured many original songs from his own heart and mind. At the time of his marriage he was in the middle stages of multiple sclerosis. They were a very insightful couple and entered marriage with the knowledge and understanding that the time they would have together would be limited.

It was one of the most unusual and wonderful weddings my wife and I have ever attended. It began with a half hour of worship music from several professional Christian musicians and lasted nearly two hours. There were also tape-recorded messages interspersed throughout the service.

For my wife and me it was a highly emotional experience, partly because of the quality of the service but also because our retarded son, Matthew, had died just two weeks before. We were in the midst of our own grief, but we wouldn't have missed this experience for anything.

Everyone who entered the church was given a bulletin that not only gave the order of the service, but background information about each participant. These descriptions were both informational and humorous. In addition, there was a piece of paper in the middle of the wedding bulletin that read:

Dear Family and Friends,

As we stated in our invitation: "Because you are the people who have touched our lives, we are asking you to participate with us and to make a commitment to be more than witnesses."

So would you please take some time to share with us some words of wisdom, a prayer, or food for thought based on an experience in your life that could help us grow, or give us guidance, as we embark upon life together?

We will be keeping all your thoughts in a notebook prepared for us, close at hand, and close to our hearts, because...

"Where there is no guidance, the people fall, but in abundance of counselors there is victory." (Proverbs 11:14)

Before and even during the service you could see individuals and couples writing their responses. By the time we reached the foyer, eighty to a hundred completed forms had been collected on a table outside the doors.

Several months later when we met with this couple, they took out a large scrapbook in which all of the responses had been pasted. They said, "Look at all this material. These are our guidelines for the first year of marriage. We take these out periodically and reread them. What a blessing they've been."

Not only were they a blessing to the couple, but each person who completed one felt as though they had truly contributed to this couple's life at the wedding service. They weren't just observers, they participated. And it was a wedding they won't forget.

How can you make your service memorable? One of the most important and helpful steps is to identify the reasons you are marrying each other. In premarital counseling I ask each person to write out twelve of these reasons. Then during the first or second session of premarital counseling the couple sits face-to-face and shares their reasons with one another. It is a crucial step to clearly identify why you are marrying this person.

I also suggest that you keep these reasons in a safe place and on your first wedding anniversary, sit together—again face-to-face—and share your reasons once again. Then, add the *additional reasons* you've discovered during your first year and why you're glad you married your spouse. Make it a yearly tradition to remind yourselves why you married one another and to celebrate newly discovered reasons.

Over the years a number of couples have incorporated their reasons for marrying into the service or vows or listed them in the wedding service bulletin. Here is a sampling:

Reasons Why (Name) Is the Right Person for Me
- We are equally yoked in our personal commitment to Christ—Jesus is number one.
- She is definitely interested in the goodwill of others—she is not absorbed into her own needs and is constantly attempting to please others above herself.

- She accepts the biblical role of marriage—the husband is to be head of the family and the wife is to support (spiritually and by validation) the husband.
- She has a forgiving spirit and accepts my shortfalls—she does not hold my shortcomings over my head, but instead is willing to work on them. She accepts me for who I am. That's rare.
- She realizes that her purpose as a mother is to raise her child in the ways of the Lord—which is evident in the manner in which she has raised (name) as a single mother.
- She accepts the financial guidelines that we have begun to introduce into our relationship. She does not argue about financial matters and does not demand material things—she's happy with the simple things.
- We are able to communicate and understand the importance of expressing our true feelings—even if it means that the other may not agree with how we feel.
- She continually keeps me on my toes with the desire to learn more about the Word of God. She is always moving forward.
- I love her: When I am in a special situation, or a special moment, she is the one with whom I want to share the moment.
- We have a special relationship, one that is not based on physical intimacies. We do not physically hang on each other all the time—we have a sense of security—knowing the other is there for us.

Reasons Why (Name) Is the Right Person for Me

- I prayed that the Lord would send me a godly man. And (name) was the person the Lord sent. He always makes sure that Christ is the center of his life—number one.
- He is always there for me to lift me up and give me encouragement, to be bolder in

my walk with the Lord—always encouraging me to become more involved.

- I think it is really important that we allowed ourselves to become friends before we started dating.

- He loves my son so much, he is very accepting of him. (Name) is always thinking of my son and always thinking of ways we can include him in the things we do.

- We have a positive line of communication.

- We love each other so much that we recognize areas in our lives that we need to work on and are willing to do so for ourselves and each other.

- He is a very compassionate and trustworthy man. He is always there to meet the needs of other people before his needs. When people need a good hug and a smile, they come looking for him.

- He is my best friend. I am able to come to him with anything and he is always there to listen, to give a hand. He never puts me down or makes fun of me. He is very helpful and patient with me. He's not condemning.

- I look forward to our times together. I can't wait to see him, and when we part I am already thinking of the next time we will be together.

- He is a very hard worker. He puts all of himself in his work to make it his best.

The following list of reasons for getting married appeared in one couple's wedding program. You will quickly see that the groom was quite a jokester. I can only imagine the bride's mother's reaction when she read it!

Top 10 Reasons for Getting Married

- She has an unexplainable draw (and it's not a southern drawl).
- I always wanted to marry a woman who drove a *truck* and still had class—and all of her teeth when she smiled.
- She's a Republican.
- She's easy to play great tricks on.
- She laughs at all my jokes (she has a great sense of humor).
- She does everything I tell her to do and likes it.
- She enjoys it when I call her my "little ball and chain."
- She enjoys me and accepts me for the goofball that I am.
- I have the utmost respect and admiration for her.
- She has an incredible capacity to love me and other people.

Creativity can also come out in wedding receptions—sometimes reducing expenses at the same time. Here's what one couple included in their wedding invitation:

> *Craig, Shelly, Asher, Julia, Kelly,*
> *Caleb and Cory hope that you will join*
> *them for an old fashioned potluck*
> *immediately following the wedding.*
> *Please bring a dish to serve 8 to 10 people to*
> *Carlson Hall before the*
> *wedding celebration.*
>
> *A-F Appetizers*
> *G-K Salads*
> *L-Z Main Dishes*
>
> *Please share our joy in Carlson Hall and enjoy the fellowship.*
>
> So continuing daily with one accord in the temple,
> and breaking bread from house to house, they ate
> their food with gladness and simplicity of heart,
> praising God and having favor with all
> people…and daily those who were being saved,
> the Lord added to the church. (*Acts 2:46-47*)

This was printed in the wedding program:

> To Our Parents,
>
> Praise the Lord, Valentine's Day is finally here! It was through God's love we met, and it is His perfect timing that brings us here today. We are happy that you are able to be here today as we commit ourselves to be husband and wife. We greatly appreciate your patience and support, especially as this day has drawn near. We cherish your friendship and invite your prayers as we enter into this institution that is as old as the Garden of Eden, yet so new to us.
>
> We thank our parents for their time and guidance through the years. From them we have learned the strength of love and the importance of family. Thank God they never gave in, let up, or broke down. They taught us important lessons to help us prepare for this day and the rest of our lives. "Mrs. Betty" and Dick and Margaret, we couldn't have made it this far without you. Thank you!
>
> In God's love,
>
> Richard and Barbara

Here's another creative idea for your wedding:

A couple married in an outdoor ceremony on a beautiful cliff overlooking the ocean in California. When the guests arrived, each couple or individual was handed a small box and asked not to open it until a certain point in the ceremony. The ceremony proceeded and when the couple said "I do," the guests were given the signal to open the lids. Out of each box flew three or four beautiful butterflies. The audience was amazed and delighted, since no one had ever experienced anything such as this. Several companies nationwide provide butterflies for wedding releases. The right cocoons are selected to hatch at a certain time, and once they do, the butterflies can live in boxes for a few days.

VOWS FOR INSPIRATION

Bride: *(Name), I love you and I am honored today to become your wife. I respect you as a man who desires the best for us, and I trust your judgment in leading me and some-day our family, as God leads us.*

I promise to remain faithful to God, seeking His will and guidance in my relationship with Him and for our marriage.

I promise to be faithful to you and above all things to honor you as my husband. I prom-ise to submit to your leadership and look forward to making our home a place of refuge for you—a home full of laughter, joy, and understanding.

(Name), I am thankful and praise God for giving me a man who loves me as you do. We've experienced many of God's blessings, and I look forward to sharing and building a lifetime with you.

I love you, (name), and am privileged to become your wife.

Groom: *(Name), when we met almost four years ago there were a lot of things I wasn't ready for—marriage was one of them. Since then, God has been at work in my life prepar-ing me for this day. The process has been long and, at times, frustrating, but it has changed my life for the better. Over those four years, without me even realizing it, you became my* *best friend. You've seen me at my best and worst, and you know my convictions and my fears.*

God has given us this gift of marriage and I now receive it. (Name), I commit my life to you, to be there when the world gets to be too much, to be someone you can count on. My desire is to rely on the Lord for His leadership and wisdom for our marriage.

Never have I been so afraid of something I've wanted so much. Afraid because I know no lifelong commitment is cheap, and this is going to cost dearly. But I am willing to pay that price for you because I know I will be gaining much more than I could ever lose.

I love you, (name), and I am filled with joy to become your husband.

Prayers and Scriptures for a Wedding Service

SAMPLE WEDDING PRAYERS

From the United Church of Christ

God the Father, God the Son, and God the Holy Spirit bless, preserve, and keep you; the Lord mercifully with His favor look upon you, and fill you with all spiritual benediction and grace, that you may so live together in this life, that in the world you may have life everlasting. (Amen.)

Let us pray—

Almighty and most merciful God, having now united this man and woman in the holy covenant of marriage, grant them grace to live therein according to your holy word; strengthen them in constant faithfulness and true affection toward each other; sustain and defend them in all trials and temptations; and help them so to pass through this world in faith toward you, in communion with your church, and in loving service one of the other, that they may enjoy forever your heavenly benediction; through Jesus Christ our Lord. (Amen.)

From the United Methodist Church

Gracious God, bless this man and woman who come now to join in marriage, that they may give their vows to each other in the strength and spirit of your steadfast love. Let the promise of your word root and grow in their lives. Grant them vision and hope to persevere in trust and friendship all their days. Keep ever before them the needs of the world. By your grace enable them to be true disciples of Jesus Christ, in whose name we pray. (Amen.)

Prayer of Thanksgiving

Minister: Friends, let us give thanks to the Lord.

People: Thanks be to God.

Minister: Most gracious God, we give you thanks for your tender love in sending Jesus Christ to come among us, to be born of a human mother, and to make the way of the cross to be the way of life. We thank you, also, for consecrating the union of man and woman in His name. By the power of your Holy Spirit, pour out the abundance of your blessing upon this man and woman in His name. Defend them from every enemy. Lead them into all peace. Let their love for each other be a seal upon their hearts, a mantle about their shoulders, and a crown upon their foreheads. Bless them in their work and in their companionship; in their sleeping and in their waking; in their joys and in their sorrows; in their life and in their death. Finally, in your mercy bring them to that table where your saints feast forever in your heavenly home; through Jesus Christ our Lord who with you and the Holy Spirit lives and reigns, one God forever and ever. (Amen.)

From the American Lutheran Church

Let us bless God for all the gifts in which we rejoice today—

Lord God, constant in mercy, great in faithfulness: With high praise we recall your acts of unfailing love for the human family, for the house of Israel, and for your people the church. We bless you for the joy which your servants (name of bride) and (name of groom) have found in each other, and pray that you give to us such a sense of your constant love that we may employ all our strength in a life of praise of you, whose work alone holds true and endures forever. (Amen.)

Let us pray for (name) and (name), that they may fulfill the vows they have made this day and reflect your steadfast love in their lifelong faithfulness to each other. As members with them of the body of Christ, use us to support their life together; and from your great store of strength give them power and patience, affection and understanding, courage, and love toward you, toward each other, and toward the world, that they may continue together in mutual growth according to your will in Jesus Christ our Lord. (Amen.)

Let us pray for all families throughout the world—

Gracious Father, you bless the family and renew your people. Enrich husbands and wives, parents and children more and more with your grace, that, strengthening and supporting each other, they may serve those in need and be a sign of the fulfillment of your perfect kingdom, where, with your Son Jesus Christ and the Holy Spirit, you live and reign, one God through all ages of ages. (Amen.)

From the Episcopal Church

Let us pray—

Eternal God, creator and preserver of all life, author of salvation, and giver of all grace: Look with favor upon the world you have made, and for which your Son gave his life, and especially upon this man and this woman whom you make one flesh in Holy Matrimony. (Amen.)

Give them wisdom and devotion in the ordering of their common life, that each may be to the other a strength in need, a counselor in perplexity, a comfort in sorrow, and a companion in joy. (Amen.)

Grant that their wills may be so knit together in your will, and their spirits in your Spirit, that they may grow in love and peace with you and one another all the days of their life. (Amen.)

Give them grace, when they hurt each other, to recognize and acknowledge their fault, and to seek each other's forgiveness and yours. (Amen.)

Make their life together a sign of Christ's love to this sinful and broken world, that unity may overcome estrangement, forgiveness heal guilt, and joy conquer despair. (Amen.)

Give them such fulfillment of their mutual affection that they may reach out in love and concern for others. (Amen.)

Grant that all married persons who have witnessed these vows may find their lives strengthened and their loyalties confirmed. (Amen.)

Grant that the bonds of our common humanity, by which all your children are united one to another, and the living to the dead, may be so transformed by your grace, that your will may be done on earth as it is in heaven; where, O Father, with your Son and the Holy Spirit, you live and reign in perfect unity, now and forever. (Amen.)

The Blessing of the Marriage
(The husband and wife kneel)

Most gracious God, we give you thanks for your tender love in sending Jesus Christ to come among us, to be born of a human mother, and to make the way of the cross to be the way of life. We thank you, also, for consecrating the union of man and woman in His name. By the power of your Holy Spirit, pour out the abundance of your blessing upon this man and this woman.

Defend them from every enemy. Lead them into all peace. Let their love for each other be a seal upon their hearts, a mantle about their shoulders, and a crown upon their foreheads. Bless them in their work and in their companionship; in their sleeping and in their waking; in their joys and in their sorrows; in their life and in their death. Finally, in your mercy, bring them to that table where your saints feast forever in your heavenly home; through Jesus Christ our Lord, who with you and the Holy Spirit lives and reigns, one God, forever and ever. (Amen.)

O God, you have so consecrated the covenant of marriage that in it is represented the spiritual unity between Christ and His church: Send therefore your blessing upon these your servants, that they may so love, honor, and cherish each other in faithfulness and patience, in wisdom and true godliness, that their home may be a haven of blessing and peace; through Jesus Christ our Lord, who lives and reigns with you and the Holy Spirit; one God, now and forever. (Amen.)

From the United Church of Canada

O God, Creator and Father of all, we thank you for the gift of life—and, in life, for the gift of marriage.

We praise you and thank you for all the joys that can come to men and women through marriage, and the blessings of home and family.

Today, especially, we think of (name of groom) and (name of bride) as they begin their life together as husband and wife. With them we thank you for the joy they find in each other.

We pray for their parents, that at this moment of parting they may rejoice in their children's happiness.

Give (name) and (name) strength, Father, to keep the vows they have made and cherish the love they share, that they may be faithful and devoted to each other.

Help them to support each other with patience, understanding, and honesty.

Teach them to be wise and loving parents of any children they may have.

Look with favor, God, on all our homes. Defend them from every evil that may threaten them, from outside or within.

Let your Spirit so direct all of us that we may each look to the good of others in word and deed, and grow in grace as we advance in years; through Jesus Christ our Lord. (Amen.)

From the Book of Common Prayer

Let us pray—

Eternal God, creator and preserver of all life, author of salvation, and giver of all grace: Look with favor upon the world you have made, and for which your Son gave His life, and especially upon this man and this woman whom you make one flesh in holy matrimony. (Amen.)

Give them wisdom and devotion in the ordering of their common life, that each may be to the other a strength in need, a counselor in perplexity, a comfort in sorrow, and a companion in joy. (Amen.)

Grant that their wills may be so knit together in your will, and their spirits in your Spirit, that they may grow in love and peace with you and one another all the days of their life. (Amen.)

Give them grace, when they hurt each other, to recognize and acknowledge their fault, and to seek each other's forgiveness and yours. (Amen.)

Make their life together a sign of Christ's love to this sinful and broken world, that unity may overcome estrangement, forgiveness heal guilt, and joy conquer despair. (Amen.)

Bestow on them, if it is your will, the gift and heritage of children, and the grace to bring them up to know you, to love you, and serve you. (Amen.)

Give them such fulfillment of their mutual affection that they may reach out in love and concern for others. (Amen.)

Grant that all married persons who have witnessed these vows may find their lives strengthened and their loyalties confirmed. (Amen.)

Grant that the bonds of our common humanity, by which all your children are united one to another, and the living to the dead, may be so transformed by your grace, that your will may be done on earth as it is in heaven; where, O Father, with your Son and the Holy Spirit, you live and reign in perfect unity, now and forever. (Amen.)

Scripture verses can be rich sources of inspiration for composing your own prayers for your future spouse and for your marriage. Here are three examples of Scripture-based prayers.

> *"It is good to give thanks to the Lord, And to sing praises to Thy name, O Most High; To declare Thy lovingkindness in the morning, And Thy faithfulness by night"* (Psalm 92:1-2 NASB).

> *O heavenly Lord,*

> *You have been good to me. You have surrounded me with Your favor like a shield (Ps. 5:12). Because of Your blessings, our family's needs are met and many of our deeper desires are satisfied (Deut. 12:7).*

> *Today I thank You for my marriage partner—the complete of my self and a continuing expression of Your goodness in my life. Thank You for making us one (Gen. 2:24), and thank You for leading us toward a deeper union despite all of our shortcomings.*

> *You have given me a friend who favors me with patience, honesty, tenderness, and good humor. Every morning I am blessed by my mate's steadying influence, hard work, and faith-*

ful shouldering of responsibility. Every evening I am comforted by our shared companionship, kindness, and affection.

Praise for You will be on the tip of my tongue all day (Ps. 34:1) because You are a generous God, and Your love for my family never stops (Ps. 136:1). I will worship You today with a contented heart (1 Tim. 6:6) because this is the marriage You have given me and the one You are ready to bless if I seek You (Ps. 119:2).

And I do!

May my attitude of gratitude be a source of strength to me all day and a source of pleasure for You (Ps. 51:12). Amen.[1]

———————

"Unless the Lord builds the house, its builders labor in vain" (Psalm 127:1).

Lord Jesus,

As we seek to create a marriage and a home together, we come to You, our Great Builder, placing our trust in the plans You have drawn for us. We know Your plans for our marriage are good, to give us hope and an exciting future (Jer. 29:11). If You build our house, we know our foundation is secure, built on solid rock (Ps. 71:3), immovable, unshakable (Ps. 46:1-2).

We trust You to build us walls of security. When the winds of trouble howl, seeking to enter through cracks in the plaster, our hearts will be secure and we will have no fear (Ps. 112:8). Even on stormy days, peace will dwell within our walls (Ps. 122:7).

We ask that Your covering of grace will be the roof of our home (Rom. 6:14). Only when we're living "under grace" can we receive one blessing after another (John 1:16).

And Lord, we ask for lots of windows—the ability to see Your beauty and respond with praise (Psalm 148)—and an open door—the gift of hospitality to strangers as well as friends (Heb. 13:1-2).

Furnish our home with lots of laughter and plenty of joy. May the walls echo with shouts of praise to You, Lord, the great builder of all things that last (Heb. 3:4).

One more thing would make our home complete. We humbly ask You to be our Honored Guest and to dwell with us all the days of our lives (Rev. 3:20). Amen.[2]

———————————

"For this reason a man will leave his father and mother and be united to his wife, and the two will become one flesh. So they are no longer two, but one" (Matthew 19:5-6).

Lord of married lovers,

Only You could defy the law of mathematics to make one plus one equal one. And that "one" is not even two halves that add up to a whole but two drastically different people who add up to an entirely new creation: Us!

We come before You in prayer on behalf of Us—a husband and wife who long to reflect Your beautiful likeness (Gen. 5:1-2) and experience the amazing oneness You promise: "Has not the Lord made them one? In flesh and spirit they are his" (Mal. 2:15).

Yet, You hear the voices, Lord, that attempt to separate Us: "Are you sure you did the right thing?" "You deserve more than this." "What if you get bored?" "Well, as long as you're happy..."

But You've shown us "the most excellent way" (1 Cor. 12:31)—cherishing our commitment as we cleave to one another (Gen. 2:24), nurturing mutual respect as we submit to each other (Eph. 5:21), finding our lives as we surrender them to You (Luke 9:24).

And this way of love will never fail (1 Cor. 13:8).

Lord of married lovers, bind us together in an everlasting covenant.

We dedicate Us to You. Amen.[3]

MARRIAGE BENEDICTIONS

(Name of bride) and (name of groom), you have now affirmed before your families and friends your love and your caring for each other. You have come from different backgrounds. You have walked different paths. You are different individuals. Your love has transcended these differences. In the years before you, may the richness of the traditions that have nurtured you enhance and brighten your lives as you help to create and shape the future.

May the challenges of your life be met with courage and optimism. May you learn from your failures and grow in your achievements. May life bless you with children, friends, and family in a wide network of mutual support and enjoyment. May you face pain, toil, and trouble with a stout but light heart. May you share with others the radiance of your seasons of joy and pleasure.

May the spirit of love be ever a part of your lives so that the union we here celebrate this day be worthy of continued celebration tomorrow and tomorrow and tomorrow. (from Kenneth W. Phifer)[4]

Most gracious God: We thank you for the beauty of this moment. Send your richest blessing upon (name of bride) and (name of groom), whom we bless in your name, that they may love, honor, and cherish each other, amid the ever-changing scenes of this life. Look favorably upon them, that their home may be a haven of blessing and a place of peace. Grant them fullness of years so that they may see their children's children. Guide them by the wise counsel of your word, and when their earthly life is complete, give them entrance into your everlasting kingdom. And now…

May God bless you and keep you.
May God's presence shine upon you
and be gracious to you
May God's presence be with you and
Give you peace.
Amen.
(from Richard Thomas)[5]

———————

By your free choice you have made a marriage.
No matter what the demands on your lives and your time,
The meaning of your living is now known through your love.
You must nurture each other to fullness
and wholeness, renew yourselves
in love and laughter, maintain the
capacity for wonder, spontaneity,
humor, sensitivity, and save time for
each other, to love each other more
deeply and learn to love more fully
the Creation in which the mystery of
love happens. Amen.[6]

You are now wed
May you always remain sweethearts, helpmates, and friends.
May your life together be full of kindness and
understanding, thoughtfulness and rejoicing.
May the years bring you happiness and contentment.
May you enter into each other's sorrow by sympathy,
Into each other's joy with gladness,
Into each other's hope with faith and trust,
Into each other's need with the sure presence of love,
Into each other's lives with enthusiasm and embracing. Amen. [7]

May your marriage bring you all the fulfillment a marriage should bring and may the Lord give you patience, tolerance, and understanding. May it be full of joy and laughter, as well as comfort and support. May you discover the true depth of love through loving one another.

Remember that every burden is easier to carry when you have the shoulders of two instead of one. When you are weary and discouraged, look to Jesus to refresh and strengthen you.

May you always need one another—not so much to fill your emptiness, as to help you to know your fullness. May you always need one another, but not out of weakness. Rejoice in and praise one another's uniqueness, for God is the creator of both male and female and differences in personality.

Be faithful to one another in your thoughts and deeds and above all, be faithful to Jesus. May you see the marriage bed as an altar of grace and pleasure. May you remember that each time you speak to one another you are talking to someone that God has claimed and told, "You are very special." View and treat your partner as one who was created in the image of God. Remember that you are not to hold your partner captive, but to give them freedom to become all that God wants them to be. May you then embrace and hold one another, but not encircle one another.

May God renew your minds so you look to draw out the best and the potential in one another. Look for things to praise, never take one another for granted, often say, "I love you," and take no notice of little faults. Affirm one another, defer to one another, and believe in your partner. If you have differences that push you apart, may both of you have good sense enough to take the first step back. May the words, "You're right," "Forgive me," and "I forgive you" be close at hand.

Thank you, Heavenly Father, for your presence here with us and for your blessing upon this marriage.

In Jesus' name,

Amen.

SELECTED WEDDING PASSAGES

Then the Lord God said, "It is not good for the man to be alone. I will make a helper who is right for him." From the ground God formed every wild animal and every bird in the sky, and he brought them to the man so the man could name them. Whatever the man called each living thing, that became its name. The man gave names to all the tame animals, to the birds in the sky, and to all the wild animals. But Adam did not find a helper that was right for him. So the Lord God caused the man to sleep very deeply, and while he was asleep, God removed one of the man's ribs. Then God closed up the man's skin at the place where he took the rib. The Lord God used the rib from the man to make a woman, and then he brought the woman to the man. And the man said, "Now, this is someone whose bones came from my bones, whose body came from my body. I will call her 'woman' because she was taken out of man." So a man will leave his father and mother and be united with his wife, and the two shall become one body. The man and his wife were naked, but they were not ashamed (Genesis 2:18-25 NCV).

God, have mercy on us and bless us and show us your kindness so the world will learn your ways, and all nations will learn that you can save. God, the people should praise you; all people should praise you. The nations should be glad and sing because you judge people fairly. You guide all the nations on earth. God the people should praise you; all people should praise you. The land has given up its crops. God, our God, blesses us. God blesses us so people all over the earth will fear him (Psalm 67 NCV).

Praise the Lord! I will thank the Lord with all my heart in the meeting of his good people. The Lord does great things; those who enjoy them seek them. What he does is glorious and splendid, and his goodness continues forever. His miracles are unforgettable. The Lord is kind and merciful. He gives food to those who fear him. He remembers his agreement forever. He has shown his people his power when he gave them the lands of other nations. Everything he does is good and fair; all his orders can be trusted. They will continue forever. They were made true and right. He sets his people free. He made his agreement everlasting. He is holy and wonderful. Wisdom begins with respect for the Lord; those who obey his orders have good understanding. He should be praised forever (Psalm 111 NCV).

Praise the Lord! Happy are those who respect the Lord, who want what he commands. Their descendants will be powerful in the land…. Their houses will be full of wealth and riches, and their goodness will continue forever. A light shines in the dark for honest people, for those who are merciful and kind and good. It is good to be merciful and generous. Those who are fair in their business will never be defeated. Good people will always be remembered. They won't be afraid of bad news; their hearts are steady because they trust the Lord (Psalm 112:1-7 NCV).

Happy are those who respect the Lord and obey him. You will enjoy what you work for, and you will be blessed with good things. Your wife will give you many children, like a vine that produces much fruit. Your children will bring you much good, like olive branches that produce many olives. This is how the man who respects the Lord will be blessed. May the Lord bless you from Mount Zion; may you enjoy the good things of Jerusalem all your life. May you see your grand-children. Let there be peace in Israel (Psalm 128 NCV).

Praise him, you servants of the Lord; praise the name of the Lord. The Lord's name should be praised now and forever. The Lord's name should be praised from where the sun rises to where it sets. The Lord is supreme over all the nations; his glory reaches to the skies. No one is like the Lord our God, who rules from heaven, who bends down to look at the skies and the earth. The Lord lifts the poor from the dirt and takes the helpless from the ashes. He seats them with princes, the princes of his people. He gives children to the woman who has none and makes her a happy mother (Psalm 113 NCV).

And now I will show you the best way of all. I may speak in different languages of people or even angels. But if I do not have love, I am only a noisy bell or a crash-ing cymbal. I may have the gift of prophecy. I may understand all the secret things of God and have all knowledge, and I may have faith so great I can move moun-tains. But even with all these things, if I do not have love, then I am nothing. I may give away everything I have, and I may even give my body as an offering to be burned. But I gain nothing if I do not have love. Love is patient and kind. Love is not jealous, it does not brag, and it is not proud. Love is not rude, is not selfish, and does not get upset with others. Love does not count up wrongs that have been done. Love is not happy with evil but is happy with the truth. Love patiently accepts all things. It always trusts, always hopes, and always remains strong. Love never fails (1 Corinthians 13:1-8, NCV).

God has chosen you and made you his holy people. He loves you. So always do these things: Show mercy to others, be kind, humble, gentle, and patient. Get along with each other, and forgive each other. If someone does wrong to you, forgive that person because the Lord forgave you. Do all these things, but most important, love each other. Love is what holds you all together in perfect unity. Let the peace that Christ gives control your thinking, because you were all called together in one body to have peace. Always be thankful. Let the teaching of Christ live in you richly. Use all wisdom to teach and instruct each other by singing psalms, hymns, and spiritual songs with thankfulness in your hearts to God. Everything you do or say should be done to obey Jesus your Lord. And in all you do, give thanks to God the Father through Jesus (Colossians 3:12-17, NCV).

I saw emptiness under the sun: a lonely man without a friend, without a son or brother, toiling endlessly yet never satisfied with his wealth—"For whom," he asks, "am I toiling and denying myself the good things of life?" This too is emptiness, a sorry business. Two are better than one; they receive a good reward for their toil, because, if one fails, the other can help his companion up again; but alas for the man who falls alone with no partner to help him up. And, if two lie side by side, they keep each other warm; but how can one keep warm by himself? If a man is alone, an assailant may overpower him, but two can resist; and a cord of three strands is not quickly snapped (Ecclesiastes 4:7-13 NEB).

VOWS FOR INSPIRATION

Bride: *I love you, (name)! I am so glad to be here today committing myself to you realizing that you are a gift from God. I'm proud of the man you've become. Your character, integrity, and commitment form a solid foundation for our relationship. Your strength and gentleness allow me to feel secure and at home with you. I treasure the fact that we laugh a lot when we're together.*

With God's help and the abilities that He's given me, I promise to make our home a peaceful place that you'll enjoy coming home to, a place of love, acceptance, and laughter!

I promise to make my relationship with you a priority, appreciating the way that our differences complement one another. With God's help, I will not run from you emotionally, knowing that you love me and that we both desire to grow through our conflicts. I will trust the Lord to guide us through the rough times as well as the easy ones. I look forward to the growth and enjoyment of living the rest of my life with you.

I am proud to become your wife today. I willingly commit myself to be your best friend, greatest fan, and exclusive lover for as long as God grants me life. I love you.

Groom: *(Name), I love you and am proud to be standing here with you before God, our family, and our friends. During the [seventeen] years we have known each other, our relationship has developed into one of those rare and valued friendships that seems to grow even* *when we're apart. It is a wonderful gift from God to base our marriage on our mutual commitment to Jesus Christ, our close friendship, and our love for each other.*

(Name), I am committed to Christ and to you. As God has called me, I will be the spiritual leader in our marriage and will rely on Him while making ours a Christ-centered home. God has given you a sensitive and gentle spirit with which to interpret this world and I will listen to your thoughts, ideas, judgment, and advice. I will seek to know and understand you so that I may better meet your needs, comfort your hurts, and communicate with you openly and honestly. You have my unreserved support, encouragement, and trust.

By God's grace and power, I will be true and faithful to you until the day that one of us lays the other in the arms of Jesus. (Name), I love you.

Quotes to Use for Your Wedding

QUOTES TO USE FOR YOUR WEDDING

The bonds of marriage are like any other bonds—they mature slowly.
— *Peter DeVries*

A successful marriage is an edifice that must be rebuilt every day.
— *André Maurois*

Marriage is that relationship between man and woman in which the independence is equal, the dependence mutual, and the obligation reciprocal.
— *Louis K. Anspacher*

The union of souls will ever be more perfect than that of bodies.
— *Erasmus*

O lay thy hand in mine dear! We're growing old; But Time hath brought no sign, dear, That hearts grow cold. T'is long, long since our new love Made life divine; But age enricheth true love, Like noble wine.
— *Gerald Masse*

Thrice joyous are those untied by an unbroken band of love, unsundered by any division before life's final day.
— *Horace*

But happy they, the happiest of their kind, Whom gentler stars unite, and in one fate Their hearts, their fortunes, and their beings blend.
— *James Thomson*

True love is a durable fire in the mind ever burning.
— *Sir Walter Raleigh*

In our life there is a single color, as on an artist's palette, which provides the meaning of life and art. It is the color of love.
— *Marc Chagall*

Love knows no rule.
— *St. Jerome*

Love is ever the beginning of knowledge, as fire is of light.
— *Thomas Carlyle*

Bitterness imprisons life; love releases it.
Bitterness paralyzes life; love empowers it.
Bitterness sours life; love sweetens it.
Bitterness sickens life; love heals it.
Bitterness blinds life; love anoints its eyes.
— *Harry Emerson Fosdick*

Oh, what a heaven is love!
— *Thomas Dekker*

Love is the only sound and satisfactory answer to the problem of human existence.
— *Erich Fromm*

I am not sure that Earth is round
Nor that the sky is really blue.
The tale of why the apples fall

May or may not be true.
I do not know what makes the tides
Nor what tomorrow's world may do,
But I have certainty enough,
For I am sure of you.
— *Amelia Josephine Burr*

Drink to me only with thine eyes,
And I will pledge with mine;
Or leave a kiss but in the cup,
And I'll not look for wine.
The thirst that from the soul doth rise
Doth ask a drink divine;
But might I of Love's nectar sup,
I would not change for thine.
— *Ben Jonson*

…come the wild weather,
come sleet or come snow,
We will stand by each other,
However it blow.
— *Simon Dach*

We loved with a love that was more than a love.
— *Edgar Allan Poe*

…Love is not love
Which alters when it alteration finds,
Or bends with the remover to remove.
O, no! It is an ever-fixed mark,
That looks on tempests and is never shaken;
It is the star to every wandering bark,
Whose worth's unknown, although his height be taken.
— *William Shakespeare*

Love's mysteries in souls do grow,
But yet the body is his book.
— *John Donne*

Our boat to the waves go free,
By the bending tide, where the curled wave breaks,
Like the track of the wind on the white snowflakes;
Away, away! 'Tis a path o'er the sea.
— *William Ellery Channing*

Thou art the star that guides me
Along life's change sea;
And whate'er fate betides me,
This heart still turns to thee.
— *George P. Morris*

Now the rite is duly done,
Now the word is spoken,
And the spell has made us one
Which may ne'er be broken.
— *Winthrop Mackworth Praed*

My fellow, my companion, held most dear,
My soul, my other self, my inward friend.
— *Mary Sidney Herbert*

Flesh of my flesh, bone of my bone,
I here, thou there, yet both but one.
— *Anne Bradstreet*

Each shining light above us
Has its own peculiar grace;
But every light of heaven
Is in my darling's ace.
— *John Hay*

Those worlds, for which the conqueror sighs,
For me would have no charms:
My only world thy gentle eyes—
My throne thy circling arms!
Oh, yes, so well, so tenderly
Thou'rt loved, adored by me,
Whole realms of light and liberty
Were worthless without thee.
— *Thomas Moore*

So thy lov'd as love is twain
Had the essence but in one;
Two distincts, division none…
— *William Shakespeare*

I think true love is never blind,
But rather brings an added light,
An inner vision quick to find
The beauties hid from common sight.

No soul can ever clearly see
Another's highest, noblest part;
Save through the sweet philosophy
And loving wisdom of the heart.
— *Phoebe Cary*

Love is not getting, but giving,
It is goodness, and honor, and peace and pure living.
— *Henry Van Dyke*

O, human love! Though spirit given
Oh earth, of all we hope in Heaven!
— *Edgar Allan Poe*

Love, all alike, no season knows, nor clime,
Nor hours, days, months, which are the rags of time.
— *John Donne*

My bounty is as boundless as the sea.
My love as deep, the more I give to thee,
The more I have, for both are infinite.
— *William Shakespeare*

Were you the earth, dear Love, and I the skies,
My love should shine on you like the sun,
And look upon you with ten thousand eyes
Till heaven wax'd blind, and till the world were done.
— *Joshua Sylvester*

The violet loves a sunny bank,
The cowslip loves the lea,
The scarlet creeper loves the elm,
But I love—thee.

The sunshine kisses mount and vale,

The stars they kiss the sea,
The west winds kiss the clover bloom,
But I kiss—thee.

The oriole weds his mottled mate,
The lily's bride of the bee;
Heaven's marriage ring is round the earth—
Shall I wed thee?
        — *Bayard Taylor*

I wonder, by my troth, what thou and I did till we lov'd?
        — *John Donne*

Two human lovers make one divine.
        — *Elizabeth Barrett Browning*

Young bride—a wreath for thee,
Of sweet and gentle flowers,
For wedded love was pure and free
In Eden's happy bowers.

Young bride—a song for thee,

A song of joyous measure,
For thy cup of hope shall be
Filled with honeyed pleasure…

Young bride—a prayer for thee,
That all thy hopes possessing,
Thy soul may praise her God and he
May crown thee with his blessing.
    — *Martin Farquhar Tupper*

One half of me is yours, the other half yours—
Mine own, I would say; but if mine, then yours,
And so all yours!
    — *William Shakespeare*

I'll love him more, more
Than e'er wife loved before
Be the days dark or bright.
    — *Jean Ingelow*

Joy, gentle friends! Joy and fresh days of love
Accompany your hearts!
— *William Shakespeare*

The fountains mingle with the river,
And the rivers with the ocean;
The winds of heaven mix forever,
With a sweet emotion;
Nothing in the world is single;
All things by a law divine
In one another's being mingle;
Why no I with thine?
— *Percy Bysshe Shelley*

Love comforteth like sunshine after rain.
— *William Shakespeare*

Love to faults is always blind,
Always is to joy incline'd,
Lawless,wing'd, and unconfin'd,
And breaks all chains from every mind.
— *William Blake*

…true love is a durable fire,
In the mind ever burning,
Never sick, never old, never dead,
From itself never turning.
— *Sir Walter Raleigh*

Love sought is good, but given unsought is better.
— *William Shakespeare*

Come live with me and be my love,
And we will all the pleasures prove,
That hills and valleys, dales and fields,
Woods or craggy mountains yield.
— *Christopher Marlowe*

…love me for love's sake, that evermore,
Thou may'st love on, through love's eternity.
— *Elizabeth Barrett Browning*

All love is sweet,
Given or returned. Common as light is love,
And its familiar voice wearies not ever.
They who inspire it most are fortunate,
As I am now; but those who feel it most
Are happier still.
   — *Percy Bysshe Shelley*

I know not if I know what true love is,
But if I know, then, if I love not him,
I know there is none other I can love.
   — *Lord Alfred Tennyson*

That Love is all there is,
Is all we know of Love…
   — *Emily Dickinson*

…Life with its myriad grasp
Our yearning souls shall clasp
By ceaseless love and still expectant wonder,
In bonds shall endure

Indissolubly sure
Till God in death shall part our paths asunder.
— *Arthur Penrhy Stanley*

Such is my love, to thee I so belong,
That for thy right myself will bear all wrong.
— *William Shakespeare*

Or bends with the remover to remove:
O, no! It is an ever-fix'd mark,
That looks on tempests and is never shaken;
It is the star to every wandering bark,
Whose worth's unknown, although his height be taken.
Love's not Time's fool, though rosy lips and cheeks
Within his bending sickle's compass come;
Love alters not with his brief hours and weeks,
But bears it out even to the edge of doom.
If this be error and upon me prov'd,
I never writ, nor no man ever lov'd.
— *Shakespearean Sonnet 116*

Shall I compare thee to a summer's day?
Thou art more lovely and more temperate…
When in eternal lines to time thou grow'st
So long as men can breathe or eyes can see,
So long lives this, and this gives life to thee.
— *Shakespearean Sonnet 18*

Then happy I that love and am beloved
Where I may not remove nor be removed.
— *Shakespearean Sonnet 25*

But here's the joy: my friend and I are one…
Then she loves but me alone!
— *Shakespearean Sonnet 42*

Thy love is better than high birth to me,
Richer than wealth, prouder than garments' cost,
Or more delight than hawks or horses be;
And, having thee, of all men's pride I boast…
— *Shakespearean Sonnet 91*

Love cometh like sunshine after rain.
— *Shakespeare*

Look down you gods, and on this couple drop a blessed crown.
— *Shakespeare*

Sensual pleasure passes and vanishes in the twinkling of an eye, but the friendship between us, the mutual confidence, the delights of the heart, the enchantment of the soul, these things do not perish and can never be destroyed. I shall love you until I die.
— *Voltaire*

It is the man and woman united that makes the complete human being. Separate she lacks his force of body and strength of reason; he her softness, sensibility and acute discernment. Together they are most likely to succeed in the world.
— *Benjamin Franklin*

O my Luve's like a red, red rose
That's newly sprung in June;

O my Luve's like the melodie
That's sweetly played in tune.
As fair art thou, my bonnie lass,
So deep in luve am I;
And I will luve thee still, my dear,
Till a' the seas gang dry.
— *Robert Burns*

There is no more lovely, friendly and charming relationship, communion or
company than a good marriage.
— *Martin Luther*

Come live with me, and be my love,
And we will some new pleasures prove
Of golden sands, and crystal brooks,
With silken lines and silver hooks.
— *John Donne*

To get the full value of joy, you must have someone to divide it with.
— *Mark Twain*

Better is a heart full of love, than a mind filled with knowledge.
— *Charles Dickens*

Friendship is a union of spirits, a marriage of hearts, and the bond of virtue.
— *William Penn*

…and yet even while I was exulting in my solitude I became aware of a strange lack. I wished a companion to lie near me in the starlight, silent and not moving, but ever within touch. For there is a fellowship more quiet even than solitude, and which, rightly understood, is solitude made perfect. And to live…with the woman a man loves is of all lives the most complete and free.
— *Robert Louis Stevenson, from "A Night Among the Pines"*

Oh, hasten not this loving act,
Rapture where self and not-self meet;
My life has been the awaiting you,
Your footfall was my own heart's beat.
— *Paul Valery*

Love is a desire of the whole being to be united to some other being.
— *Samuel Taylor Coleridge*

Love is like a mirror. When you love another you become his mirror and he becomes yours…And reflecting each other's love you see infinity.
— *Leo Buscaglia*

Love, like a lamp, needs to be fed out of the oil of another's heart, or its flame burns low.
— *Henry Ward Beecher*

I like not only to be loved, but to be told I am loved.
— *George Eliot*

All the beautiful sentiments in the world weigh less than a single lovely action.
— *James Russell Lowell*

In pleasure's dream, or sorrow's hours,
In crowded hall or lonely bower,
The business of my soul shall be
Forever to remember thee!
— *Ben Franklin*

There is no remedy for love but to love more.
— *Henry David Thoreau*

Love seeks one thing only: the good of the one loved. It leaves all other secondary effects to take care of themselves. Love, therefore, is its own reward.
— *Thomas Merton*

Beyond
Beyond words or phrases or prose penned
Beyond the lines and meter and rhythm and rhyme
Beyond a syllable whispered or sound released
Language cannot reach the place where your love has carried me
— *Pam Farrel*

Love is an irresistible desire to be irresistibly desired.
— *Robert Frost*

Two persons must believe in each other,
And feel that it can be done and must be done;
In that way they are enormously strong.
— *Vincent Van Gogh*

Nothing wastes more energy than worrying.
The longer one carries a problem, the heavier it gets.
Don't take things too seriously.
Live a life of serenity, not a life of regrets.

Remember that a little goes a long way.
Remember that a lot…goes forever.
Remember that friendship is a wise investment.
Life's treasures are people…together.

Realize that it's never too late.
Do ordinary things in an extraordinary way.
Have health and hope and happiness.
Take the time to wish upon a star.

And don't ever forget…
For even a day…how very special you are.
— *Collin McCarty*

A good relationship has a pattern like a dance and is built on some of the same rules.

The partners do not need to hold on tightly, because they move confidently in the same pattern, intricate but gay and swift and free,
like a country dance of Mozart's…

There is no place here for the possessive clutch, the clinging arm,
the heavy hand; only the barest touch in passing.

Now arm in arm, now face to face, now back to back—it does not matter which.

Because they know they are partners moving to the same rhythm,
creating a pattern together and being invisibly nourished by it.
— *Source Unknown*

How could anything rightly be said about love if You were forgotten,
O God of love, from whom all love comes in heaven and earth;
You who held nothing back but gave everything in love;

You who are love, so the lover is only what he is through being You?
— *Soren Kierkegaard*

> A happiness that is sought for ourselves alone can never be found: for a happiness that is diminished by being shared is not big enough to make us happy.
>
> There is a false and momentary happiness in self-satisfaction, but it always leads to sorrow because it narrows and deadens our spirit. True happiness is found in unselfish love, a love which increases in proportion as it is shared.
> — *Thomas Merton*

Love is a gift
    from out of the stars and into your hearts
    from each of you to the other:
    from who you are and who you become to the
    wider circle of family and friends
    who are your community;
    from each child and parent and caring friend
        to you, (name of bride) and (name of groom)
Love is a gift, a magnificent mystery.

Love is a hard-earned treasure
    wrenched from the depths of mortal self-centeredness,
    at risk in every open and unspoken conflict;
    part of the struggle to give to the other without giving yourself away;
    endlessly demanding of you both repentance and forgiveness;
    every day asking something of you to prove you
    are worthy of the grace of such a caring relationship;
Love is a hard-earned treasure, a genuine moral achievement.

Love is a joy
    making your eyes light up
    and sometimes fill up;
    giving you laughter to uplift your souls;
    bringing you intense pleasure
        at the sound of your beloved's voice
        at the very touch of a hand
        or lips sweetly embracing;
    lifting you from despair and loneliness
    to companionship and meaningfulness;
Love is a joy, the richest blessing you can know.

Love is a communion
    of your unity with each other;
    of your relation to those who are part of

your circle of caring,
    children and relatives and friends;
of your feelings for each other
    focused in this special moment but enduring
    through the past,
    in the present,
    and into the future;
of our feelings for you
    as we have known you,
    as we know you now,
    as we will know you in the days ahead;
of your ties to the earth,
    to the air and water and fire,
    to worms and winged creatures and wolverine,
    to woman and man,
    to life itself;

Love is a communion, the circle within which we all
live and move and have our being.
(Name of bride) and (name of groom);
May all that you are always be in love;
May all that is love always be in you.
May your love be as beautiful on each day you share
As it is on this day of celebration.
    — *Ken W. Phifer*[1]

The meaning of marriage begins in the giving of words. We cannot join ourselves to one another without giving our word. And this must be an unconditional giving, for in joining ourselves to one another we join ourselves to the unknown. We can join one another only by joining the unknown. We must not be misled by the procedures of experimental thought: in life, in the world, we are never given two known results to choose between, but only one result that we chose without knowing what it is.

Marriage rests upon the immutable *givens* that compose it; words, bodies, characters, histories, places. Some wishes cannot succeed, some victories cannot be won, some loneliness is incorrigible. But there is relief and freedom in knowing what is real, these givens come to us out of the perennial reality of the world, like the terrain we lie on. One does not care for this ground to make it a different place, or to make it perfect but to make it inhabitable and to make it better. To flee from the realities is only to arrive at the unprepared.

Because the condition of marriage is worldly and its meaning communal, no one party to it can be solely in charge. What you alone think it ought to be, it is not going to be. Where you alone think you want it to go, it is not going to go. It is going where the two of you—and marriage, time, life, history, and the world—will take it. You do not know the road; you have committed your life to a way.

— *Wendell Berry*[2]

If your love is to grow and deepen,
you must find a way to move
with each other;

perhaps in a slow and graceful dance
(bare feet firmly feeling the ground),
a dance, that circles and tests
and learns
as it gradually moves closer
to that place
where you can each
pass through the other
and turn and embrace
without breaking
or losing any part of yourselves
but only to learn more of who you are
by your touching,
to find that you are each whole
and individual and separate
yet, in the same instant,
one, joined as a whole
that does not blur the two individuals
as you dance.

The music is there
if you will listen hard,
through the static and noise of life,
and other tunes that fill your heads.

You are here,
marking time to the music.
The dance can only begin
if you will take the first (and hardest)
tentative,
uncertain,
stumbling
steps.

    — *Paul L'Herron*[3]

When you love someone you do not love them all the time, in exactly the same way, from moment to moment. It is an impossibility. It is even a lie to pretend to. And yet this is exactly what most of us demand. We have so little faith in the ebb and flow of life, of love, of relationships, it will never return. We insist on permanency, on duration, on continuity; when the only continuity possible, in life as in love, is in growth, in fluidity—in freedom, in the sense that the dancers are free, barely touching as they pass, but partners in the same pattern.

The only real security is not in owning or possessing, not in demanding, or expecting, not in hoping, even. Security in a relationship lies neither in looking back to what it was in nostalgia, nor forward to what it might be in dread or anticipation, but living in the present relationship and accepting it as it is now. For relationships, too, must be like islands, one must accept them for what they are here and now, within their limits—islands, surrounded and interrupted by the sea, and continually visited and abandoned by the tides. One must accept the security of the winged life, of the ebb and flow, of intermittency.

— *Anne Morrow Lindbergh, Gift from the Sea*[4]

I do not offer the old smooth prizes,
But offer rough new prizes,
These are the days that must happen to you;
You shall not heap up what is called riches,
You shall scatter with lavish hand all that you earn or achieve.
However sweet the laid-up stores,
However convenient the dwellings,
You shall not remain there.
However sheltered the port,
And however calm the waters,
You shall not anchor there.
However welcome the hospitality that welcomes you

You are permitted to receive it but a little while
Afoot and lighthearted take to the open road,
Healthy, free, the world before you,
The long brown path before you, leading wherever you choose.
Say only to one another:
Carerado, I give you my hand!
I give you my love, more precious than money,
I give you myself before preaching or law:
Will you give me yourself?
Will you come travel with me?
Shall we stick by each other as long as we live?
  — *Walt Whitman*[5]

To love is good; love being difficult. For one human being to love one
another; that is perhaps the most difficult of all our tasks, the ultimate, the
last test and proof, the work for which all other work is but preparation.
For this reason [beginners] cannot yet know love: they have to learn
it…Learning-time is always a long, secluded time, and so loving, for a long
while ahead and far on into life, is—solitude, intensified and deepened
loneness for him who loves…it is a high inducement to the individual to
ripen, to become something in himself, to become world, to become world
for himself for another's sake, it is a great exacting claim upon him, something that chooses him out and calls him to vast things. Only in this sense,

as the task of working at themselves ("to hearken and to hammer day and night") might young people use the love that is given them.

— Rainer Maria Rilke[6]

Romantic love is eternally alive; as the self's most urgent quest, as grail of our hopes of happiness, as the untarnished source of the tragic, the extreme and the beautiful is modern life. The late twentieth century is the first to open itself up to the promise of love as the focus of universal aspirations....

In the marriage ceremony, that moment when falling in love is replaced by the arduous drama of staying in love, the words "in sickness and in health, for richer, for poorer, till death do us part" set love in the temporal context in which it achieves its meaning. As time begins to elapse, one begins to love the other because they have shared the same experience....Selves may not intertwine; but lives do, and shared memory becomes as much of a bond as the bond of the flesh....

Family love is this dynastic awareness of time, this shared belonging to a chain of generations....We collaborate together to root each other in a dimension of time longer than our own lives.

— *Michael Ignatieff, "Lodged in the Heart and Memory"*

God with honour hang your head,
Groom, and grace you, bride, your bed
With lissome scions, sweet scions,
Out of hallowed bodies bred.

Each be other's comfort kind:
Deep, deeper than divined,
Divine charity, dear charity,
Fast you ever, fast bind.

Then let the march tread our ears:
I to him turn with tears
Who to wedlock, his wonder wedlock,
Deals triumph and immortal years.
— *Gerard Manley Hopkins, "At the Wedding March"*

…Still I am prepared for this voyage, and for anything else you may care to
    mention.
Not that I am afraid, but there is very little time left.
You have probably made travel arrangements, and know the feeling.
Suddenly, one morning, the little train arrives in the station, but oh, so bit!
…Now we are both setting sail into the purplish evening.
I love it! This cruise can never last long enough for me.

…Ribbons are flung, ribbons of cloud

And the sun seems to be coming out. But there have been so many false
    alarms…

No, it's happened! The storm is over. Again the weather is fine and clear…

And the voyage? It's on! Listen everybody, the ship is starting,

I can hear its whistle's roar! We have just time enough to make it to the
    dock!

And away they pour, in the sulfurous sunlight,

To the aqua and silver waters where stands the glistening white ship

And into the great vessel they flood, a motley and happy crowd

Chanting and pouring down hymns on the surface of the ocean…

Pulling, tugging us along with them, by means of streamers,

Golden and silver confetti. Smiling, we laugh and sing with the revelers

But are not quite certain that we want to go—the dock is so sunny and
    warm.

That majestic ship will pull up anchor who knows where?

And full of laughter and tears, we sidle once again with the other
    passengers.

The ground is heaving under foot. Is it the ship? It could be the dock…

And with a great whoosh all the sails go up…

…Into the secretive, vaporous night with all of us!

Into the unknown, the unknown that loves us, the great unknown!

    — *John Ashbery, "The Skaters"*

When our two souls stand up erect and strong,
Face to face, silent, drawing nigh and nigher,
Until the lengthening wings break into fire
At either curved point, —what bitter wrong
Can the earth do us, that we should not long,
Be here contented? Think. In mounting higher,
The angels would press on us and aspire
To drop some golden orb of perfect song
Into our deep, dear silence. Let us stay
Rather on earth, Beloved—where the unfit
Contrarious moods of men recoil away
And isolate pure spirits, and permit
A place to stand and love in for a day...

— *Elizabeth Barrett Browning, Sonnets from the Portuguese, Sonnet XXII*

That I may come near to her, draw me nearer to thee than to her; that I may know her, make me to know thee more than her; that I may love her with the perfect love of a perfectly whole heart, cause me to love thee more than her and most of all. Amen. Amen.

That nothing may be between me and her, be thou between us, every moment. That we may be constantly together, draw us into separate loneliness with thyself. And when we meet breast to breast, my God, let it be on thine own. Amen. Amen.

— *Temple Gairdner, prayer before his marriage*

My true love hath my heart and I have his,
By just exchange one for another given;
I hold his dear and mine he cannot miss;
There never was a better bargain driven:
My true love hath my heart and I have his
My heart in me keeps him and me in one;
My heart in him his thoughts and senses guides;
He loves my heart for once it was his own;
I cherish his because in me it bides:
My true love hath my heart and I have his.

 — *Sir Philip Sidney, "My True Love Hath My Heart"*

Love me little, love me long
Is the burden of my song;
Love that is too hot and strong, burneth all to waste;
Still I would not have thee cold,
Or backward or too bold,
For love that lasteth till 'tis old
Fadeth not in haste…

 — *Anonymous*

If ever two were one, then surely we.
If ever man were lov'd by wife, then thee;
If ever wife was happy in man,
Compare with me ye women if you can
I prize thy love more than whole Mines of gold,
Or all the riches that the East doth hold.
My love is such that Rivers cannot quench,
Nor ought but love from thee, give recompence.
Thy love is such I can no way repay,
The heavens reward thee manifold I pray.
Then while we live, in love let's so persever,
That when we live no more, we may live ever.
— *Anne Bradstreet, "To My Dear and Loving Husband"*

Come live with me and be my love,
And we will all the pleasures prove
That hills and valleys, dales and fields
And all the craggy mountains yield.

There we will sit upon the rocks
And see the shepherds feed their flocks,
By shallow rivers to whose falls
Melodious birds sing madrigals

And I will make thee beds of roses
With a thousand fragrant posies,
A cap of flowers and a kirtle
Embroidered all with leaves of myrtle.

A gown made of the finest wool
Which from our pretty lambs we pull;
Fair lined slippers for the cold,
With buckles of the purest gold;

A belt of straw and ivy buds,
With coral clasps and amber studs:
And if these pleasures may thee move,
Come live with me and be my love.

The shepherds' swains shall dance and sing
For thy delight each May morning:
If these delights thy mind may move,
Then live with me and be my love.
     — Christopher Marlowe, "The Passionate Shepherd to His Love"

You are my [husband/wife]
My feet shall run because of you.
My feet, dance because of you.
My heart shall beat because of you.
My eyes, see because of you.
My mind, think because of you.
And I shall love because of you.
— *Eskimo love song*

May the road rise up to meet you.
May the wind be always at your back.
May the sun shine warm on your face,
The rain fall soft upon your fields.
Until we meet again, may God
Hold you in the palm of his hand.
— *Irish blessing*

VOWS FOR INSPIRATION

Groom: *(Name), I love you and I will forever love you. Being led by God I choose you today to be my wife and rejoice in the opportunity to be your husband. I accept you just as you are and receive you as God's precious gift to me. By God's grace and power I commit to love and respect you, placing your needs before my very own. I will celebrate your strengths and encourage you in your weaknesses, always striving to see the best in you.*

I promise to support you in our ministry together as we seek to know God more intimately every day and to make Him known to the ends of the earth. I will faithfully pray for you every day. I will be there for you in every situation as a lifelong companion and friend. It is my desire to grow every day in loving you and laying my life down for you following the example of Christ. Other men may choose differently, but for me and my house we will serve the Lord. Sweetheart, I love you and before God who made this union possible and our family and friends, I pledge to you my faithful love that will last for all eternity.

Bride: *(Name), it is with a heart full of love and devotion that I come to you today. Being led by God, I rejoice in the opportunity to be your bride and choose you to be my husband, accepting you as you are and receiving you as God's precious gift to me. I will stand with you through every circumstance that comes our way, through adversity and trials and through the joyful and triumphant times. I will celebrate your strength and encourage you in your weaknesses, always striving to see the best in you and placing your needs before my own.*

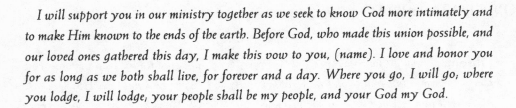

I will support you in our ministry together as we seek to know God more intimately and to make Him known to the ends of the earth. Before God, who made this union possible, and our loved ones gathered this day, I make this vow to you, (name). I love and honor you for as long as we both shall live, for forever and a day. Where you go, I will go; where you lodge, I will lodge; your people shall be my people, and your God my God.

Endnotes

I Promise

[1] Rebecca Cutter, *When Opposites Attract* (New York: Dutton, 1994), 189, adapted.

[2] Charlie Shedd, *Letters to Philip: On How to Treat a Woman* (Garden City, NY: Doubleday and Company, Inc., 1968), 82-83, adapted.

[3] H. Norman Wright, *Finding Your Perfect Mate* (Eugene, Ore.: Harvest House, 1995), portions adapted.

[4] Donald Harvey, *The Drifting Marriage* (Grand Rapids, Mich.: Fleming H. Revell, 1988), 213.

[5] Harvey, 214-15, adapted.

[6] Mike Mason, *Mystery of Marriage* (Portland, Ore: Multnomah Press, 1985), 34.

[7] Daphne Rose Kingma, *Weddings from the Heart* (New York: MJF Books, 1991), 14.

[8] Mason, 78-79, 113, 120.

[9] Lewis Smedes, *How Can It Be All Right When Everything Is Wrong?* (New York: Harper & Row, 1982), 54.

[10] Mason, 142.

[11] Jerry and Barbara Cook, *Choosing Love* (Ventura, Calif.: Regal Books, 1982), 78-80.

[12] David Augsburger, *Sustaining Love* (Ventura, Calif.: Regal Books, 1988), 72.

[13] Daniel Levinson, *The Seasons of a Man's Life* (New York: Alfred A. Knopf, 1978), 245-46.

There's More Than One Way to Tie the Knot

[1] Taken from a message by Gary Richmond, First Evangelical Free Church of Fullerton, California.

[2] William Shakespeare, *The Plays and Sonnets of William Shakespeare*, vol. 2 (Chicago: University of Chicago, 1952), 75.

[3] Shakespeare, 295.

[4] Max Lucado, *And the Angels Were Silent* (Portland, Ore.: Multnomah Press, 1992), 82.

[5] Susan Lane and Sandra Carter with Ann Scharffenberger, *Reaffirmation* (New York: Harmony Books, 1982), 140-42, adapted.

What Could Possibly Go Wrong?

[1] Robert Fulghum, *It Was on Fire When I Lay Down on It* (New York: Dillard Books, 1988), 12-13.

Reaffirmation of Your Vows

[1] Susan Lane and Sandra Carter with Ann Scharffenberger, *Reaffirmation* (New York: Harmony Books, 1982), 14.

[2] Lane and Carter, 62.

[3] David Viscott, *I Love You, Let's Work It Out* (New York: Simon & Schuster, 1987), 279, 281, 283-84.

[4] Used by permission of the author, John C. Bonser, of Flourissant, Missouri.

[5] Taken from *Treasury of Wedding Poems, Quotations and Short Stories* (New York: Hippocrene Press, Inc., 1998), 42-43.

Prayers and Scriptures for a Wedding Service

[1] David and Heather Kopp, *Praying the Bible for Your Marriage* (Colorado Springs: Waterbrook Press, 1998), 111.

[2] Kopp, 29.

[3] Kopp, 27.

[4] Taken from *For as Long as We Both Shall Live*, Thomas Roger Fritts (New York: Avon Books, 1993).

[5] Fritts, 73.

[6] David A. Johnson, *To Love, Honor and Shave Twice a Week* (Brookline, Mass.: Philomath Press, 1989).

[7] Johnson.

Quotes to Use for Your Wedding

[1] Taken from *For as Long as We Both Shall Live*, Thomas Roger Fritts (New York: Avon Books, 1993).

[2] Wendell Berry, *Standing by Words* (North Point Press, Farrar, Straus and Giroux, Inc.).

[3] Taken from *For as Long as We Both Shall Live*, Thomas Roger Fritts.

[4] Anne Morrow Lindbergh, *Gift from the Sea* (New York: Pantheon Books, 1955).

[5] Taken from *For as Long as We Both Shall Live*, Thomas Roger Fritts.

[6] *Letters to a Young Poet*, translation by M.D. Herter Norton. This quote and the quotes following are taken from *Wedding Blessings*, with an introduction by Eleanor Munro (New York: Penguin Books, 1989), various selections.

A Place to Record

Your Vows as a

Keepsake

OUR VOWS

Date

A PLACE TO RECORD YOUR VOWS AS A KEEPSAKE